GOD SAID, "HA!"

GOD SAID "HA!"

Julia Sweeney

BANTAM BOOKS

New York   Toronto   London   Sydney   Auckland

GOD SAID, "HA!"

A Bantam Book / July 1997

All rights reserved.
Copyright © 1997 by Julia Sweeney

BOOK DESIGN BY GLEN EDELSTEIN

Visit the *God Said, "Ha!"* Web site @ www.godsaidha.com

Library of Congress Cataloging-in-Publication Data
Sweeney, Julia.
God Said, "Ha!" / Julia Sweeney.
p.   cm.
ISBN 0-553-10647-3
1. Sweeney, Julia—Health.   2. Cervix uteri—Cancer—Patients—United States—Biography.   3. Women comedians—United States—Biography.   4. Actresses—United States—Biography.   5. Cervix uteri—Cancer—Patients—United States—Family relationships.   I. Title.
RC280.U8S92   1997
362.1'9699466—dc21

[B]
                                                                                    97-3019
CIP

Published simultaneously in the United States and Canada

Bantam Books are published by Bantam Books, a division of Bantam Doubleday Dell Publishing Group, Inc. Its trademark, consisting of the words "Bantam Books" and the portrayal of a rooster, is Registered in U.S. Patent and Trademark Office and in other countries. Marca Registrada. Bantam Books, 1540 Broadway, New York, New York 10036.

PRINTED IN THE UNITED STATES OF AMERICA
BVG   0 9 8 7 6 5 4 3 2 1

To Mike

My life closed twice before its close;
  It yet remains to see
If Immortality unveil
  A third event to me,

So huge, so hopeless to conceive,
  As these that twice befell.
Parting is all we know of heaven,
  And all we need of hell.

—EMILY DICKINSON

ACKNOWLEDGMENTS

A very special thanks to Greg Kachel, who directed the original production of *God Said, "Ha!"* beginning in January 1996 at the Magic Theater in San Francisco, and beginning in June 1996 at the Coronet Theater in Los Angeles.

I would also like to thank my editor, Emily Heckman, who persevered with me while I learned to make the transition from monologue to written word.

And then I want to specially thank Kathleen Murphy and Richard Jameson, two of the best writers anywhere. Fortunately, they are two of my best and dearest friends. They were constantly encouraging, loving, and sympathetic, and taught me how writers think.

Thanks, thanks, thanks goes to: Jon Steingart, the producer of my monologue in San Francisco, Los Angeles, and New York; and Beth Lapides and Greg Miller of the Uncaberet at Luna Park, where I first started doing my material.

Additionally, I would like to thank:

Fred Allen, Robin Berlin, Thom Biggart, Michelle Carter, Toby Corbett, Jim Emerson, Dave Fox, Carl Frank, David Frank, Mark Friedman, Jim Freydberg, Rebecca Gilchrist, Wendy Goldman, The Groundlings, Michael Hole, Mame Hunt, Paul Kachel, Connie Martin, Frier McCollister, Beth Milles, Frank Miraglia, Gavin Palone, Raul Porras, Roslyn Portnoy, Seth Rothschild, Jeff Rowlings, Pete Tangen, Quentin Tarantino, Mary Zophres.

Of course I have a deep-felt thanks to my parents, Bob and Jeri Sweeney, and to my brothers and sister, Bill, Meg, and Jim Sweeney. So many relatives were incredibly helpful too, I just have to mention them: Bonnie and Tom Brunton, Shirley and John Rutz, Pat and Cathy Ivers, Tom Ivers and Marie Ivers and Todd Ivers.

And I love Mike's dear friends, too numerous to mention. But especially, Dave August, Sharon Hall, Tom Reynolds, Cheri Oteri, and Andy Nicastro.

CONTENTS

PROLOGUE   xi

1. The Rock   1
2. Orange Sherbet   7
3. Nunsense   14
4. My Shangri-la   25
5. Brothers in L.A.   28
6. Mike Is Sick   31
7. Mom Rant   36
8. Dad Rant   43
9. Food   49
10. Sleeping Arrangements   51
11. The Feline Response   56
12. Pat Is Mayor for the Day   64
13. Radiation   76
14. The Threshold of Hope   80

15.	In a Lonely Place	88
16.	Carl	92
17.	I Love My Shunt	98
18.	I Know Where I'm Going	100
19.	Sympathy Cancer	104
20.	Dr. Fu	107
21.	House Guest	112
22.	International House of Cancer	117
23.	The Long, Long Drive	120
24.	Mike Gets Sicker	126
25.	Heaven Is an Instant	129
26.	Hysterectomy	135
27.	A Dozen Eggs	141
28.	Motherhood Deferred	145
29.	Mom and Dad, Go Home!	155
30.	Fire-stop	158
31.	Sister Antonella	160
32.	Lost Ovaries	163
33.	Jesus and the House Is Empty	165
34.	Taking the Rock Back	168
POSTSCRIPT		172
PICTURE NOTES		173

PROLOGUE

Hi. I'd like to introduce myself. I'm Julia Sweeney.

This may seem unnecessary, considering my name is on this book, and you might remember me from being a cast member on *Saturday Night Live* for four years, where I became known for playing "Pat," who is this drooly, creepy, large androgynous character. I also occasionally appeared on the show looking like myself, which was fun too, although sometimes it was even more scary than appearing as Pat.

Anyway, this character became so popular that Disney made a film for me to star in as Pat. And during the summer that *It's Pat* was being released (which was my last season on *Saturday Night Live*), MTV asked me to cohost the Summer Vacation Countdown of videos, which was going to be shot in Hawaii, a place I'd never been.

Okay, call me nuts, but I never wanted to go to Hawaii. I'd never been and never planned to go. Why? First of all, there's all that sun. Sun, sun, everywhere. I've just never been a big sun person. It could be genetic, since my skin seems to have been made for a rainy forest in Ireland. My skin feels great when it gets four, maybe five or six sunny days a year; any more than that and my epidermis feels like it's being slapped by the sun and it screams to me: "What are you thinking?" I feel like a polar bear in the tropics.

For another reason, it seems customary in sunny places to wear less clothing. Don't get me wrong, I'm not ashamed of my body, I just don't see any reason to not cover it up as much as possible. I'm one of those people who think those garments the Amish women wear are a great idea for everyone, regardless of their religious affiliation. I'm someone who considered becoming a nun, for the outfits.

Okay, there's more. Here comes the truth. I was supposed to cohost the MTV countdown with the regular host, Daisy Fuentes. And Daisy is this tall, voluptuous, part Cuban woman whose skin does not say to her that it was made for a rainy forest in Ireland. And I was to stand next to Daisy Fuentes wearing a bathing suit.

Let me just put it this way: Bathing suit manufacturers give Daisy bathing suits to wear because . . . well, because when Daisy is wearing a bathing suit, the last thing you notice is the bathing suit. And I guess for bathing suit companies, that's a good thing.

At first I tried to convince the MTV people that it would be funnier if I was dressed as Pat. In a bathing suit. I figured I could get around the androgynous angle by wearing one of the 1920s wool one-piece unisex bathing suits.

But they didn't go for that. They wanted me. As me. In a bathing suit. Next to Daisy.

Okay. All right. Breathe. It'll be fun. Breathe. It'll be fine. I accept. Inside, I couldn't help but feel that sinking insecurity.

Since I knew that a total physical transformation was unlikely to take place in a few weeks, my mind searched for some type of psychological strategy to get me through this daunting job. And then I remembered something. Long before I became a comedienne, I was listening to this NPR interview with Françoise Gilot, the artist and former lover of Pablo Picasso. I was working away at my desk, doing my accounting job (more about that later) listening to the radio. The interviewer asked Françoise, "Why do you think Picasso was so attracted to you?" and I thought, *Why should* she *answer that? What is she supposed to say? How awkward!*

But to my surprise, Françoise happily responded. She said, "Vell, he vas acttracted tooo me becuz I was very very butte-e-fowl und very, very intel-ee-gente.'' Just like that. She said she was beautiful and intelligent. So matter-of-factly. I couldn't stop laughing.

Fortunately for Ms. Gilot, she was and is very beautiful and intelligent. For her, this is a fact, plain and simple.

So I decided to adopt her attitude whenever I needed, you know, a little boost in my own self-confidence.

For example. Once I was performing on a show as Pat. And I was in my fat suit and my getup: the eyebrows, the wig, the whole nine yards. And I was lingering in this waiting area, waiting for my scene to be shot. There were lots of actors there, and extras, and stagehands—pretty much everyone who wasn't working at that minute was in this holding area.

And there was this actor there who I'd seen in a lot of movies. He's very handsome and roguish, in a very black leather/swagger/cigarettey kind of way. I thought he was cute.

But he was a big flirt too. And he was flirting with everybody. And by the way he was flirting, you could tell his type immediately—tall, very thin, lots of thick hair, and their lipstick had to be pouty. But I was attracted to him and he wasn't giving me (or Pat, really) the time of day.

So that's when I decided to call on good old Françoise. I immediately put myself into that "I am beautiful and intelligent" frame of mind, and when I do this, it's hard not to think with a very thick French accent. And not to think that I was not only Pablo Picasso's lover, but also the wife of Dr. Jonas Salk, who developed the polio vaccine. So I turned toward this actor, and started to radiate Françoise like crazy. I wouldn't have been surprised if I were mouthing the words "I am beautiful. I am intelligent." Now let me tell you, I wasn't even sure if this actor knew that I didn't normally look like Pat. To him, that was probably the real me.

So I kept channeling Françoise and glancing toward him. And the damnedest thing happened.

I swear to you this guy suddenly stopped talking to all of these women who were hovering around him and he started to stare at me. And I looked away, as if I were bored.

But he kept looking at me. Then he got up, practically knocking this one girl off the arm of his chair, and he came over to me and sat down. And I looked at him playfully and said, "Having a good time, Mr. Popularity?" And he blushed, and I could tell that although he was creeped out by my appearance, he was also totally intrigued. We talked for an hour and he asked for my number. And then they called me to the set and as I walked away, I could tell that he was really weirded out by the fact that he was attracted to me.

And I loved it.

So, I remembered this and decided that I could do this show with Daisy and I said yes to MTV and got on a plane and went to Hawaii.

And just as I thought, Daisy really is a statuesque goddess whose breasts hit me just at eye level, so the cameramen have to keep doing all of this clever framing and ingenious camera-angle work. We spent two days traipsing in the sand together in front of the cameras. I was saying things like "Hey, Counting Crows can really sing it!" And "What about Aerosmith?" or "Stay tuned for another one from Janet Jackson." And I think only one of my lines came out in a French accent.

But Daisy and I laughed through the entire shoot, and I was thinking how really nice and funny she was (I mean, she even leaned down for the camera, so my face wasn't right in her chest).

Surfers and beach bunnies were strewn all over the beach with their tan bodies and hair all big and stringy from the salty sea.

And that's when I had this great moment. It was like an out-of-body experience where I feel like the world is suddenly in black and white. And there's a camera on a really tall crane that is moving farther and farther away from me and it's way up over me. And I'm this tiny, tiny thing way down there. And in this moment, I love the feel of the sun on my arms and legs. It is warm and glowing, and it washes everything in a light that makes everyone and everything so appealing. And I feel so lucky to be there in just that instant.

It almost feels like I'm in the middle of some film God is making about my life.

Yup. Life just isn't too bad if you can pull off a little attitude adjustment.

Thanks, Françoise.

Chapter 1
THE ROCK

WHEN I FINALLY LEFT *SATURDAY NIGHT LIVE,* I really needed a vacation. If nothing else, on that show, you work very very hard. Well, maybe not as hard as a person with three children who has two jobs. That person would really need a vacation. Or, if you were a slave building the pyramids in ancient Egypt. Those guys really needed a vacation.

But even still, I thought I deserved a vacation, too. I was coming off a four-year job that had totally engulfed my life. I was free and clear. I had saved my money! The future was a blank. Anything could happen! I had no responsibilities!

My friend Quentin invited me to accompany him to the Nottingham Film Festival in England. Quentin had directed a movie that appeared to be promisingly popular, and it was going to be featured there. For me, this trip was going to be nothing but fun, and relaxing.

Quentin and I met up in London and then we headed to Nottingham. Or "Not-in-am," as the locals say.

Naturally everyone at the festival thought I was Quentin's girlfriend, which I'm not, and we were having to continually explain this to people. This sort of clarification is never quite believed, that you are just friends: man and woman, traveling together. They either think one of you is in love with the other, or suppressing it, or some very sad and unnatural platonic ritual is being carried out between you that couldn't possibly be intimacy without the accompanying nakedness. And this was all compounded by the fact that girls were besieging Quentin—girls of the film festival groupie variety who wanted to spar with him verbally, to show their independent strong wills, their Katharine Hepburn–like coltishness, and their knowledge of the nuances of cinema verité.

Finally, we gave up and didn't explain ourselves to anyone. It was no use.

The best thing about Quentin, in the male friendship department, is that he is as attentive and protective of me as he would be if he WAS a boyfriend. He'll always know where I am in a room, or if I've wandered off or am getting bored, or really need to eat or really really can't stay for the midnight movie, 'cause we've already seen FOUR movies today.

Anyway, it was awfully fun getting to be with my friend, whose movie was beautifully received. Once the film festival ended, we headed to the Emerald Isle for some real rest and relaxation.

We were going to stay with two of my favorite people, Cheryl and Michael, who at the time were living half the year in New York City and half the year in Ireland. My ''heritage'' is Irish, in that American green-beer-on-St.-Paddy's-Day kind of way. The way that has nothing to do with the real Ireland at all.

I suddenly found myself in the most beautiful and relaxing place on earth. It was lush green everywhere; it seemed like the vegetation was just growing, growing, against its will.

Cheryl and Michael were magnificent hosts. They were calm and doting, and they had food out everywhere for nibbling. Naps were encouraged, conversation was the art, and strolling through the hills was our exercise. Their house was perched on a ridiculously picturesque spot. Stone fences outlined the green pastures, and cow upon cow, lamb upon lamb greeted you continually as you walked. Plump Cheshire cats draped themselves over stone fences and you rarely heard the crackle of the gravel to alert you that a car was approaching. When it did, the driver waved.

I carried around a biography of Yeats and threw myself, haphazardly and impetuously, anywhere I wanted and read another chapter. My body felt like it was home.

Cheryl and Michael had seven cats, so I, a major cat lover, was immediately making their acquaintance and getting to know their various personalities and hearing all their tales of woe.

As Cheryl and I had predicted, Quentin and Michael totally hit it off and the chattering went on for four days. I'm bad at remembering the hilarious conversations we had. So I have no way to prove to you how funny Michael was. All I know is that at one restaurant, Michael said something to me that made me laugh so hard that my drink came out my nose. And that hasn't happened since I was seven.

One day we decided to take a boat to a small island off the coast. This island is called Inish Turk. The island is basically deserted, although, at one time, it had nearly 250 people living on it. But with the coming of electricity, there was no way to get the electric cables over the ferocious Irish Sea to Inish Turk, so people moved ashore few by few. So that now the island is littered with the remains of stone fences and long-abandoned homes. Cows still roam free on the island and you come across the occasional cat.

Quentin and I wandered off to explore the island. We went over to the far side, the side facing the Atlantic. The shoreline is rugged and abrupt, and white rocks are piled against the coastline and are mercilessly whacked by the water, day after day. Thousands, millions, zillions of small white stones, about two inches in diameter, wedge themselves along the sand, making it look like cobbled snow.

Quentin and I walked way out onto the rocks, looking out at the empty sea. He picked up a rock and said, ''I'm going to keep this rock. It's going to be my lucky rock. I'll always have it and it will always remind me of this time.'' In a moment of adoring little sisterhood, I blurted out, ''Me too, I'm going to have to find my lucky rock too.''

So I found myself my rock. Small, perfectly white, a little tinge of moss on the underside. Quentin and I clacked our bits of stone together and put them in our pockets.

On the way back, in the boat, we told Cheryl about our lucky rocks. She said, ''You know the curse, don't you? They say that for anyone who takes a rock off an island off the coast of Ireland, misfortune lies ahead.''

We ignored her and kept the rocks.

Chapter 2
ORANGE SHERBET

WHEN I WAS SIX I COMMITTED MY FIRST CRIME. It was a Saturday afternoon—that time when, oh, just a year or so before I would have been bedding down for a nap, but now I was big and I didn't have to take a nap, so I had this time on my hands. Well, I was walking down the upstairs hallway in our house, and as I passed my parents' bedroom, I happened to notice my mother's purse open and kind of just lying there, willy-nilly, on the bed. And suddenly it became irresistible to me and I decided I wanted to steal something from it, and that something was money.

So I went in and I took out her wallet and I had to calculate exactly how much I could take without her noticing and I figured that that would be about a dollar fifty. One paper bill and two quarters. Perfect. So I put the money into my pocket and I walked back out into the hallway and suddenly it felt like it was really bulging out of my pants. It was this hot money and I felt I had to get rid of it right away. I had to flee the scene. Fast.

So, I went downstairs to the family room and turned on the TV and sat down on the ottoman. And I tried to watch that TV but I couldn't because of the money. I felt like it was heating up in my pocket.

Fortunately, I had just been given permission to cross the street on my own. So, I decided to do so, and I walked over to the corner market where we shopped. I walked in and said hi to the grocer, who knew me and my whole family. I walked past him really fast because I didn't want him to see that my face was so red and how I had to lift my right leg up while I walked to hide all that money in my pocket.

I walked up and down the aisles and I tried to think of something that would be just right and would take up almost all of the dollar fifty. And since six-year-olds don't usually stroll around a grocery store on their own, just browsing, I had to act fast. I made my way down each row, following the one rule I made up for this search—if I passed something, I couldn't go back for it. I slowly considered each food item and stepped forward. Finally, I found myself in front of the freezer in the back, and my eyes came to rest on the perfect thing. A gallon of orange sherbet.

I grabbed my orange sherbet and I headed up to the cash register and I paid for it, acting really casual. I even told the grocer to keep the rest of the change because I didn't want any of that hot money on me, even though I'd just exchanged most of it for this gallon of orange sherbet. But he said he couldn't keep the change (can't you tip your grocer?) and I was thinking to myself that this wasn't good—that maybe for the thirteen cents of change he would keep his mouth shut about this little incident.

I was seriously sweating at this point, and since I was in such a hurry to get out of there, I declined a bag and headed for home.

Then I started walking home, hugging this huge, cold and sticky cardboard cylinder to my chest, and something suddenly occurred to me: *Oh my God, where am I going to hide it?*

So I got back to my house and I snuck up the driveway. The garage door was open. So I bolted for its safety and crouched down in the cool darkness of the garage, sure that no one had seen me. Then something else occurred to me: *Oh my God—this orange sherbet is going to melt!*

Now I really had to start thinking fast.

So I snuck back into the house and went to the kitchen and just as I was about to grab the biggest spoon I could find, my mom called out from the dining room, "Julie?" And I said, "I'm sorry, I'm busy right now." And I got a spoon and I ran back out to the garage and I started eating that orange sherbet. And it tasted really really great.

After I'd eaten about a third of the gallon, I was pretty much full. So I left that huge container of sherbet in the garage and decided to go out to the backyard—as if I'd find a way out of this huge jam I was in back there. And I did. My brother Michael was playing alone in the sandbox just behind the garage.

Mike was about three at this time. So I went up to him and said, "Hey, Mike, come over here." And he came over and followed me back to the garage. Then I said, "Look. It's your favorite, orange sherbet," and Mike said, "Yeah!"

Now, I wasn't exactly sure if this *really* was his favorite, but my psychology worked because Mike started eating and eating the orange sherbet. He got it all over his face and all over his hands and he became this orange sherbet eating machine. And he didn't stop until the entire gallon was finished.

The carton was empty, but Mike was a vision in orange. So I looked around the garage and I saw some paper towels that my dad kept in there and I used them to wipe up his face and his hands and I was really proud of myself because, you know, here I was thinking of all the angles. So I got Mike, who was now sort of a silent partner in the whole affair, cleaned up, and I hid the evidence behind some tools at the back of the garage. Since it was almost dinnertime, we headed back to the house.

We went in through the back door and were cutting through the kitchen and who's standing there? My mother. She sort of cocked her head to the side and put her hands on her hips (the international sign for maternal omniscience) and said, ''Hey, where have you two been?'' And we said, ''Nowhere.'' And she said, ''Are you sure you don't want to tell me anything about anything?'' And I said, ''No, we've just been playing under the swing set trying to dig a hole to China or something.'' And she said, ''Now are you sure you don't want to tell me something?'' We said, ''No,'' both of us looking down as though we were actually able to see China through the linoleum.

And at just that moment, Mike opened his mouth and out started coming the orange sherbet.

It was like a fountain! It went onto his knees and onto the floor. It was like one of those scenes from a Roman

Polanski movie where the plumbing breaks and it just over-flows and overflows and there's no end in sight. And Mike looked up at me with these big eyes like, ''I can't believe I blew it.'' It was such a poignant look and I'll never forget that look.

Ironically, years later when Mike was eighteen, he started his own ice cream business. He got his own truck and he had freezers installed inside and he even negotiated with Carnation Ice Cream in Spokane, Washington, where we lived, for inexpensive ice cream.

He had the sides painted with the logo ''Oasis Ice Cream'' (although I have no idea why he named it that) and the prices and he had a state-of-the-art sound system put into it. But instead of the usual deedle dee deedle dee (you know—the unforgettable and classic ice cream truck theme music), Mike chose to play Van Halen's ''Ice Cream Man.''

A lot of Mike's best business was conducted down at Comstock Park, which was kind of a stoner hangout. And a lot of times the teenagers would come up to the truck and say, ''Hey, Mike, bong hit for a Creamsicle?'' And depend-ing on Mike's mood, sometimes he would agree to that transaction. Mike the ice cream man. He was good at it and his business was very successful.

But there was a problem with this moneymaking scheme of Mike's. And that was that there already was a really solidified ice cream–selling cartel in the area. Almost like a kind of Ice Cream Mafia. And they really didn't like it that Mike was suddenly in their territory. And Mike told me that once they even tried to drive him off the road. And when he told me about it he laughed and said, ''You should have heard it, Jules, that deedle dee deedle dee ramming into the Van Halen. It was beautiful.''

Chapter 3
NUNSENSE

DOUGLAS FAIRBANKS THEATRE   ADFTNN111693E
432 WEST 42ND STREET
NUNSENSE   50%OFF
                              $16.25
8:00 PM TUE   BWYEVE TE
NOV 16, 1993
RATKTS103 1116 0100D00009   ORCH
REDUCED PRICE
NOT FOR RESALE   B   15

SUBJECT TO TERMS AND
CONDITIONS ON REVERSE SIDE.

ONCE I BECAME AN ADULT, I would usually see my parents for about two or three weeks a year. I would always go home during Christmas for a week and then they would come visit me for another week during the year wherever I was living, and that would usually be Los Angeles or Manhattan, depending on where I was working. I felt we were spending just the right amount of time around each other.

Now, my parents, who had spent almost all their growing-up time in small communities, really like the fact that I've chosen to live in big metropolises. They especially love New York City, where my mother's always saying things like, "You can just feel the energy coming up through the sidewalks!!!'' And then she'll wave her hands over her head to represent the energy.

Whenever they'd come to visit me, I would always have to guide them around and show them things, but at the same time be deferential, because, you know, they're my parents. It's a tricky dance that we're always dancing.

Three years ago, when I was living in New York City and working on *Saturday Night Live,* my parents came for their annual visit. I was working so hard that I didn't really have time to mull over what kinds of fun things we could do together, and I was feeling a little stressed out that I didn't have an itinerary put together for them. But fortunately, I'd been invited to this restaurant opening that a chef friend of mine was having. I knew there'd be lots of atmosphere, and free food and excitement. So I invited my parents to go along with me and I told them to be ready at the apartment on that day at about 7:30, that I would probably have to work right up until that time, but I would come home and get them and we would go on to the opening.

Well, the day of our big night out arrived, and as I was leaving Rockefeller Center, I looked at my invitation and realized that I had mixed up the date of the opening—it had already happened. The day before. Damn. I realized I had to think up something else QUICK.

So, I got back to the apartment and there my parents were, standing by the door, all dressed up, with their coats over their arms. I swear to God they look a foot shorter in New York City.

I said to them, "Mom, Dad. I'm terribly sorry but we're going to have to make a change in plans." And they sort of murmured in unison, "Oh, a change of plans," and sat down on the bed. I explained to them that I had mixed up the night of the restaurant opening, that it had been last night. But I was prepared to suggest an alternate plan. "How about we go to the same restaurant, have a nice long leisurely dinner, my treat? And then afterward, if we feel like it, we can go to the video store and pick up a video and come back to the apartment and watch it?"

Well, then my mother, because she insists on being contrary to me at all times, said, "No, I would like to see a Broadway show. I'm dressed to see a Broadway show. Let's go see a Broadway show."

"Oh," I said. "Well, it's 7:40. And you see, Broadway shows start at 8:00 . . ."

My mother did not see this as a problem.

She said, ''All right, we have twenty minutes. And what's playing on Broadway and what do you think I'd like and what's available?''

And I said, ''Oh, well, I don't really have that information off the top of my head. But I do know that in Times Square they have this *half-price* ticket-selling booth where they sell tickets to shows that aren't sold out. And maybe if we rushed there we could get something . . .''

Oh, they liked that: *half price!*

So, we went downstairs and out onto the street and miraculously we got a cab right away. And my mother immediately leaned across the seat and said to the driver, sort of confidentially, ''Hi, my name is Jeri Sweeney. And this is my husband, Bob Sweeney. And we're here all the way from Spokane, Washington, visiting our daughter who's in show business. And we would like it if you would take us to Times Square where they sell those half-price tickets at the last minute to Broadway shows and . . . then . . . wait for us there while we decide what theater we'd like to go on to.''

I then had to explain to my mother that first, the cab-driver couldn't understand anything she had just said, and second, it was not exactly appropriate to ask a cabdriver to wait for you at ten to eight in Times Square while you decided what theater you're going to go to. (This would be like asking mission control at NASA to "hold that shuttle" while you made a quick trip to the bathroom.)

So the cab dropped us off and we rushed up to the booth and I realized I had to explain the half-price ticket rules to my parents in record time. "Mom, Dad, here's a list of the plays. If there's a line through it, it means the play is sold out and unavailable. If there's not a line through the play, it means it's available. So let's just choose a play."

My mother looked up and she said, "Well I would like to see the *Sisters Rosenshweeg*." And I said, "Oh, okay, well, first of all it's *Sisters Rosensweig,* but second of all, it's unavailable because, as you can see, there's a line through it."

And then she blurted, "Oh, *NUNSENSE* IS PLAY-ING!!!"

"Oh . . . . . . *Nunsense,*" I said.

"You know"—she was exhilarated now—"your father and I saw that in Ashland and it is hysterical."

"Well, you know, I really have no interest in seeing *Nunsense*. However, I am interested in seeing ANY of the other plays that are available, of which, as you can see, there are many,'' I replied.

''Oh really?'' she said. ''Because your father and I—we thought it was *hysterical*.''

And I said, ''Well, you've seen it, and I haven't seen it, so it seems like everyone's happy. Maybe we could just choose something else.''

Then my mother lowered the tone of her voice about an octave and said, ''I said it was hysterical.''

At just that moment the man behind the booth shouted out, ''We're closing, last call!'' And my mother rushed up and she said, ''We want three tickets to the *Sisters Rosenshweeg*.'' And the guy growled, ''Well, lady, that's unavailable.'' And I whispered, ''Yes, Mother, as I told you, that's unavailable.''

My mother paused to collect herself and then she burst out in a brisk staccato, like it was coming from somewhere else, somewhere deep inside her: ''Oh . . . NUN-SENSE!''

So that's how we came to have three tickets to *Nunsense*.

Now, I can't explain to you exactly why I didn't want to see *Nunsense* so much. But I think it has something to do with my fear of Catholic vaudeville. And my feeling that there might be a lot of big wacky nuns running around the stage throwing rosaries out at us. And well, frankly, I was afraid that I would be offended, even though I'm not a practicing Catholic. My parents, well, they're big practicing Catholics.

But here we were, with three tickets to *Nunsense,* and my mother said, "Well, where's the theater?" And I said, "It's on Fortieth and Tenth." And she said, "Is that a long way away?" And I said, "Yes it is. It's a long way away. It's a long long way away."

So we started walking. I was walking like a block ahead and I was so angry. And they're scurrying behind me trying to keep up. We got to the theater at one minute to eight and, well, there were plenty of seats available.

The ushers kind of herded us all down to the first three rows. My parents and I were sitting in the middle of the second row. Immediately, the lights went down and the play started and it was just as I feared. There's the big, chubby, singing Carmen Miranda nun, and the tall, athletic, homely nun and then there's the beautiful, quiet and sweet, the how-did-SHE-become-a-nun? nun. And they were, in fact, throwing rosaries out at us and holy water and holy cards.

I looked over at my parents. All the blood had rushed to their heads and they were rocking back and forth. They were laughing harder than I had literally ever seen them laugh in my entire life. To them, this was the funniest play they'd ever seen.

So, you know, I tried. And I watched and scrutinized and I kind of became the Margaret Mead of observing nuns. And then, right in the middle of the second act, the big Carmen Miranda nun stopped the entire show, looked right into the audience and said, ''Hey! I think we have a celebrity in the audience! Isn't that Pat from *Saturday Night Live*!?'' And my mother said, ''They know you! They know you!!!'' And I looked up at the stage, and the Carmen Miranda nun shouted out, ''Would Pat be a priest or a nun?'' And everyone went, ''Hahahahaha!''

And I wanted to just die. But my parents were beaming. And I thought, *God bless them, they are so proud of their daughter that it doesn't matter that this character, that Pat, is completely unattractive and a freak. They are still tickled that I would get recognized in an off-Broadway theater with twenty people in the audience.* The singing Carmen Miranda nun quickly lost interest in Pat, to my great relief, because it was the part in the show where they sprayed the audience with holy water.

The play finally came to an end. And I was woozy from this experience, like I was seriously swaying. Before we'd barely made it out into the lobby, my mother was pulling on my sleeve and asking, "So, what did you think?"

"Well, it was a little derogatory in its portrayal of nuns, don't you believe?" I said.

Now I was thinking about all of the wonderful orders of nuns that I've known of and read about, who've done such incredible work here, and in Central and South America, and, well, all over the world, really. And even the sisters who taught me in grade school and high school, and what intelligent, prideful educators I found them to be. And especially Sister Antonella, my favorite English teacher in high school, who taught me so much about literature and life. I guess that's why I was kind of offended that nuns were being portrayed on the stage in this manner.

Then my mother chirped, "Well apparently Cardinal Mahoney seems to like it."

She then referred to this big blown-up article that was in the lobby of the theater. It was an article that I was sure my mother thought was a review, but was in fact not a review. It was this article from *The New York Times* that said, basically, "Wow, isn't it amazing that *Nunsense* is still playing in New York after ten years?"

And sure enough, in the body of this article, Cardinal Mahoney had put in his two cents and said how *hilarious* the play is. Mahoney being one of the many misogynistic cardinals in the Catholic Church.

I looked at this and I said, ''Oh, that's perfect, that's just perfect. You know, Mother, I don't think these cardinals would think this play was quite so hilarious if it were about a bunch of bumbling, half-witted . . . priests!''

At just that moment my father turned to me and he said, ''You know, Julie, I think you're committing the sin of pride right now.''

So that night, as soon as I got home, I got out my copy of St. Thomas Aquinas's *Summa Theologica,* because he was the first Catholic to write extensively about the Seven Deadly Sins and I thought I would look up this sin of pride, which I had apparently, just hours before, committed. As it turned out, Thomas Aquinas had a really interesting take on the sin of pride. His idea was that you could commit the sin of pride by, well, by being arrogant—but you could *also* commit the sin of pride by . . . like, not living up to your potential. The idea being that God has given you these certain gifts and if you don't use these gifts then you're committing the sin of pride.

I read that, and I thought, wow, that Thomas Aquinas, he was really cool and really evolved way back in the thirteenth century. So I kept reading and it was pretty great until I came upon a chapter entitled "Why Are Women Born?"

I suppose he's posing the question biologically.

Thomas Aquinas, given the medical knowledge that he had available to him in the thirteenth century, wrote:

> Weakness of seed or unsuitable material are not the only causes for females to be conceived. There are also external circumstances, such as the direction of the wind or an idea in the mind at the time of intercourse.

Oh, comforting. One of the things that I love about the Catholic Church are the hilarious gems of the absurd tucked in amongst some truly insightful concepts. Ah, religion.

Chapter 4
MY
SHANGRI-LA

DURING MY THIRD YEAR ON *SATURDAY NIGHT LIVE,* my husband and I split up. It was an amicable breakup. In fact, we used to joke that it was a divorce made in heaven.

We were good friends and decided to honor that friendship by continuing it outside of the messy context of a marriage. It took us a long time to decide to break up and it was sad and painful.

But there was one thing I really looked forward to, and that was the chance to live alone again. I saved my money diligently while I was working, and I finally had enough for a down payment on a little bungalow in Hollywood. I made it my symbol of independence. For the first year that I had this house, I was still living in New York City and I scrimped and saved and sent my money back home so that I could decorate it. I wanted to make sure that it was really girlie, and strongly feminine. And I wanted to make sure that it said to anyone who walked in: "A woman lives here. Alone. And happy about it!"

I developed this elaborate fantasy for my Shangri-la. I believed that I would spend a lot of time alone there and I would give a lot of petite soirees and fabulous gourmet dinner parties. And there'd be lots of witty talk.

Maybe someone would drink a little bit too much. And I would insist that they spend the night in the guest room, a perfectly charming place to crash after an evening of rousing conversation. We'd be up late into the night talking about oh, say, the latest Coen Brothers movie, or maybe the problems in Bosnia with that horrible Slobodan Milosevic. Or we could all play a fun game where we name all the Justices on the Supreme Court. And everyone would just love the dessert I'd made, and someone would inevitably say, "This pie is fabulous, and aren't blueberries even out of season?"

I figured that I would spend long afternoons listening to Tchaikovsky and writing all those great screenplays that are just floating around in my head. Days would be spent like my vacation in Ireland, except all the time and every day. Brilliant minds would leisurely lounge around my house, laughing uproariously at someone's ingenious bon mot. We'd all hang out around the barbecue in the afternoon and at night we'd all drink sherry and smoke Cuban cigars.

I would never marry again! I would live in this house alone! Gloriously alone for the next sixty years! Well, me and my three cats: Gus, Rita, and Frank.

And after a few years, my neighbors would look down the street and they would say to their friends, ''There lives Julia Sweeney. You know, she never remarried after a brief early liaison, but we've never known anyone who was happier and more full of life than that Julia Sweeney! How we envy her existence!''

I could see all of this happening as I organized my bedroom and picked out fabric for curtains and scoured antiques fairs for end tables. I was finally an independent adult! I felt so mature and self-reliant. I had gone to college, I'd started my career, I'd even had the big wedding, and that BIG relationship. But nothing was more exciting to me now than having my own place.

And that's when God just said . . . ''Ha!''

Chapter 5
BROTHERS IN L.A.

Two of my brothers, Mike and Jim, also lived in L.A. It was pretty cool that even though Spokane is twelve hundred miles away, I would still get the benefit of having two of my siblings and me living in the same city again.

Jim, my youngest brother, works for the Mayor of the City of West Hollywood. He majored in Government in college and then got an internship in the city's office.

Mike, who moved to Los Angeles about five years before, worked selling tickets at The Universal City Amphitheater, then worked as a counter clerk at Thrifty Auto Rental in Beverly Hills. And then he came to work at The Groundlings Theater, running the box office. I was performing at the theater then, and occasionally doing accounting work in the business office, so we got to see each other a lot. Which was great.

Somehow, Mike lived like a king on nothing. He had always been a master of getting things for less than anyone else. Mike would clip out coupons from the Thursday food section in the *L.A. Times* and then comparison shop for mayonnaise and shampoo. But then he'd treat himself to elaborate trips. He had taken a train across the country three times. He went to Santa Fe, to Mexico, to Hawaii, which he loved. He knew how to get rental cars for a pittance and drive to Las Vegas, where he knew where all of the best twenty-dollar-a-night hotels were and he'd have half-price tickets for the shows. Mike belonged to the Omaha Steaks' ''Steak-of-the-Month'' Club, and the *Gilligan's Island* Episode-of-the-Month fan club. And every Sunday Mike and Jim would eat brunch at The Pantry downtown. Mike enjoyed things.

Mike moved into my old apartment, after I had moved into a bigger apartment in the same building. He used my washer and dryer and gave me tips on inexpensive laundry detergent that you only had to drive an extra two miles to get. We cohosted parties together, including one humongous, ten-hour-long Thanksgiving dinner.

When I bought my house, it was sad not to live right next door to Mike anymore.

About a month after I moved back from New York and I had just begun to settle into my new, perfect little home, I got some terrible news. My brother Michael was diagnosed with lymph cancer.

Chapter 6
MIKE IS SICK

MIKE HADN'T BEEN FEELING WELL FOR A WHILE and he didn't have any insurance, so he would go to the free clinic. Mike's symptoms and profile (single man, thirty years old) seemed to lead all of the doctors to one possible diagnosis, and Mike was given one HIV test after another, and he always tested negative. They didn't keep searching for anything else.

Mike was experiencing all kinds of weird things—his left leg would go numb, his chin was numb, his teeth would ache. He was terribly tired all the time. His stomach hurt, too.

I learned of all this later. Mike didn't tell me a thing about his symptoms. I later heard that he had asked people not to tell me, not to mention it. He figured it would go away, and he probably knew that I would make a big deal about it.

He just kept going to the free clinic and to the occasional dentist, what could be wrong?

In late July, he went ahead with his plans to visit his friend Sharon in Rochester, New York. He and Sharon were old pals and had been ''Thanksgiving'' buddies for years. Mike took off for his trip and while in a restaurant in Rochester he passed out and was rushed to the hospital.

My brother Jim called with the news. He said Mike was in the hospital. Diagnosis: ulcer. The news was upsetting but not catastrophic.

I talked to Mike immediately and he seemed embarrassed for having passed out in public and glad that they had found the ulcer. Maybe he would finally stop having such a bad stomachache. He also complained about the nurses. Surly, he said. The doctors in Rochester had decided to do more tests, however. Family phone calls became conferences and we were all so relieved that Mike finally knew the cause of his aches and pains. Mike didn't want anyone to fly out. He was okay. He'd be out of the hospital in a few days and

GOD SAID, ''HA!''

back in L.A. soon enough. He had to eat a special diet for the ulcer, that was all.

"Don't come! Don't come!" he insisted.

Mike had no insurance, but the hospital couldn't refuse him as an emergency patient. Sharon was running the gamut of forms and regulations and appeals to help keep him there. One day there became four, five, six. Eventually the tests the doctors had ordered became conclusive. Mike had lymphoma. Stage four. And there only are four stages.

My father immediately flew out to Rochester. And Mike wasn't happy about it: He wanted to be left alone, and he felt he could communicate with us via the phone—but this wasn't okay with my dad and he went to the airport immediately. My mother and I soon followed.

I got us a hotel room that was like a suite, sort of a hotel apartment, and we immediately set up camp. Mom, Dad, Jim, my brother Bill, who lives in Spokane, and I were there on and off for six weeks. Mike was sick. Really sick.

They had given him an enormous dose of chemotherapy. It seemed to be unraveling the tumors but with lymphoma it's tricky—lymph systems interact, if you will, and the devilish cancer could be anywhere, everywhere. Based on Mike's age and condition, he had a forty percent chance of recovery. We thought these odds were beatable. I looked at it like a class that you had to get into the top forty percent of in order to graduate. Easy.

But chemo kills cells, not just cancer cells. The bet with chemo is that the cancer cells won't grow back and the healthy ones will replace themselves. This is a layperson's description of chemo, but we did basically come to understand that the whole point of it was to make you sicker and then make you better. It's kind of like dropping a neutron bomb into your body and then hoping that you have a kick-ass, internal Red Cross crew ready to pick up the pieces. Mike and I referred to the chemo as Drāno.

Mike wasn't doing well. One of his doctors there told Mike he was the sickest patient in the cancer ward. Another said, ''Are you religious?'' When Mike looked up at him, surprised, the doctor said, ''If I were you, I would start praying.''

I guess that's a prescription, in a way.

I just stayed for the duration once I got to Rochester because it seemed right that I should be away from Hollywood and with my brother. The Pat movie had opened the weekend before I learned of Mike's illness. It opened in two theaters in Seattle and Houston. It got terrible reviews. No one attended. It was closed in a week.

It was a big painful lesson, releasing that movie. And too bad too, because it had been an absolute joy to make. And I was so proud of it. But it immediately became water under the bridge. Here I was in Rochester with Mike, who was so sick. Suddenly the movie seemed tiny and puny.

After five weeks the doctors said that Mike could probably return to L.A. the next week. I went back first to see what hospital or doctor we could get him hooked up with. Mike accepted my offer to move in with me—just temporarily—and until he could get back on his feet and feel well enough to be alone in his apartment again. Jim flew home with Mike a few days later.

So Mike moved in and Jim was over all the time and helping out.

And before a few weeks were up, my parents, who were, naturally, distraught, packed up all of their bags, drove down from Spokane, and moved in. The catastrophic nature of the situation was slowly sinking in. People were bringing multiple suitcases.

And, for the next nine months, there we all were in my perfect little house made for one.

Chapter 7
MOM RANT

LET ME JUST TAKE A *MOMENT* TO RANT TO YOU about what it's like to suddenly have your parents move in with you when you've spent half your life living away from them. And they're there because of an awful crisis. You find that you can never really lose your temper because of the enormity of the whole situation.

I mean, I love my parents. I really really do. But family members have idiosyncrasies that we all can find to be charming when you see them for two weeks out of the year; after that, they begin to seriously test your endurance—especially when you're exposed to those traits on a daily basis.

For example, this is how my mother would answer the phone: "Hello, this is Jeri Sweeney answering the telephone to take down a message for her daughter, Julia Sweeney."

I had to take her aside and say, "You know, hello. That would be fine."

My mother also has this habit of stringing together disconnecting thoughts and trying to present them as one idea. She's always saying things like, "Oh, I think that cantaloupe would work, the blouse you wanted altered is on the bed, have you seen the car keys?" Once my mother said to me, "You know I think your father might be getting Alzheimer's, because he doesn't know what I'm talking about half the time."

My mother has this storytelling technique that I call "The Red Herring" style. She'll drop a piece of very intriguing unrelated information into the top of her story and then go on and act as if it's irrelevant. She'll say something like, "I had to go to the grocery store to get the ingredients for that potato salad and oh, I had a hard time getting out of the driveway because there was a man lying there. But anyway, I couldn't remember if you like the Idaho potatoes or . . ."

And then I'll say, "Um . . . There was a man . . . lying in my driveway?" And then she'll always act as if I've interrupted the cadence of her story, and she'll say, "Oh, uh, um, yes."

Since my house is rather small, I tore down an old shed and I built a small office in my backyard, so I could have a quiet place to work and where I could experience that sensation of "going to the office." This is where I write and prepare for auditions, or, as my mother calls them, my "tryouts."

Well, I would be in my office working and my parents seemed to always be coming back and asking me questions and just generally interrupting me. Finally, I had to explain to them that when they did that, it was like not only having my parents with me in my house, but it was like having my parents with me at my job, too. And so they agreed they would only come back there if it was really, really important, something that sort of reached "emergency" on the situation scale.

So my mother immediately came back and she said, "Julie, I'm sorry to bother you, but I have been through your kitchen top to bottom and I cannot find where you keep your mixes." And I said, "My what?" And she said, "Your mixes. You know, like your Laura Scudder's Beef Stroganoff mix. Where is that?"

Another time she came back and she said, "Julie. I'm sorry to bother you, but the light has gone out in the bathroom and I found another bulb, but I didn't know if you wanted it screwed in in some special way.''

My mother also has her own special way of doing the laundry. She does all sorts of loads, lots of small delicate-cycle loads, and there are always lots of things just ''soaking'' in the washer, not being washed per se, but just kind of *sitting* there.

And then the drying. Everything is predetermined to dry at a rate that cannot be achieved by the dryer, for some reason. And so clothing is strewn all over the house, over chairs, over doors, on doorknobs, so it can go through the crucial and final stage of drying—the evaporation process—which usually takes a few hours.

My mother also has a thing about elevators. I discovered this while we were at the hospital in Rochester, where we took elevators many, many times a day. My mother would always act as if she were seeing an elevator for the first time, that it was some kind of miracle invention and she would react with awe whenever we approached one. Every single time.

I'd find myself sort of sharing in her wonderment. We would wait expectantly for the elevator. And when it arrived, we would:

1. Share a look of surprise and excitement at what
    an incredible world this is: Look! The elevator has ar-
    rived!

2. Then I would rush in first and immediately press the
    OPEN button . . . because my mother, not yet over
    her excitement at this marvelous new invention, would
    have to compose herself and then prepare herself to get
    in. And this takes a certain amount of time.

3. Finally, she would leap over the chasm between the
    hallway and the elevator proper. A leap. And I mean a
    leap. As if the elevator were going to suddenly rush
    away from her.

Once we were both on the elevator, I would press the button of the floor we were going to, and then we would have
to share many glances back and forth at each other and up at
the lit-up numbers above us as they changed. Because it was
just all so incredible.

My mother is from that generation where they believe
that doctors know everything about everything.

We'd be in a hallway in the hospital, and we'd be coming out of the office of the lymph cancer specialist. And he
would have just given us a lot of information that is really

somewhat confusing, but mostly scary, and on top of that, very very technical. And we'd see a group of doctors. (We'd know because they were all men and they kind of looked like stockbrokers, except they were wearing white instead of blue pinstripes.)

At that moment my mother would say, ''There are some doctors. Maybe you should go ask THEM about lymph cancer.'' And I would look at her like she'd just arrived from Mars. But she'd go on: ''I just tracked down the number of Dr. Moore, you know, my old OB-GYN? And I was thinking that maybe you should call him and ask him what HE knows about lymph cancer.''

And I would say, ''You know, I don't think that your gynecologist, who retired ten years ago, will know that much more about lymph cancer than one of the foremost authorities on lymph cancer here at the UCLA Cancer Center and who we just talked to.''

And this is from the woman who, when I was fourteen and had walked proudly into the kitchen and exclaimed, ''I'm going to marry a doctor,'' said to me, ''Don't marry a doctor. *Be* a doctor.'' And that was such a cool and perfect and true and progressive and gutsy response. And that has rung in my head my whole life. Don't marry a doctor, *be* a doctor. And while I didn't end up in the medical profession, I always used that as my own personal version of the "Be All That You Can Be!" motto. Only, I didn't join the army, or go to medical school, though around this time, I was wishing that I had. And that I'd studied a lot about lymphoma.

Chapter 8
DAD RANT

MY FATHER WAS AN ASSISTANT U.S. ATTORNEY for about thirty years, and after his retirement five years ago he decided to spend all of his new free time listening to National Public Radio. He has a little Walkman that he keeps on his belt and these headphones. And like a stereotypical teenager in a movie, he's always off in his own little world. Recently he told me that he hasn't missed *Morning Edition* once in seven years. And because of this it seems as though Bob Edwards, and Nina Tottenberg, and Cokie Roberts are his very best friends.

I think he has this special fondness for Cokie because he'll always say things like, ''Oh. Do you know what Cokie did today?'' And then he'll grab his abdomen and chuckle. Or he'll say, ''Cokie doesn't like what that Bob Dole is saying.''

Or one time he said to me, ''You know Cokie broadcast in her pajamas today.''

And I said, ''Really?''

And he said, ''Yeah, they set up this broadcast equipment right in her home, so she could just get up and broadcast, and this morning she said she was in her pajamas. Can you imagine?''

And I said, ''Oh, Cokie!''

Now, because my father was constantly listening to NPR (and I mean constantly—like he listens to it all night, because there's a special Canadian broadcast between the hours of 3:00 and 5:00 A.M.), we always knew the news, you know, as it was happening.

One day my father came bounding down the hallway and he said, ''Julie, there's been an earthquake in Japan!''

And I said, ''Oh, when?''

And he said, ''Thirty seconds ago!''

Now, we were especially concerned about this because my sister Meg lives in Tokushima, Japan, which is only forty miles from Kobe, the earthquake's epicenter. Meg has lived there for seven years and she has a Japanese boyfriend, whose name is Yamamoto, and he's a sweet-potato farmer. She calls him Yam for short. And since he doesn't speak any English, he doesn't know how funny that is.

My parents continually tried to call Meg after they heard about the quake, but all the phone lines were jammed. Finally, after an hour and a half, they got through. Meg answered the phone, and my mother immediately grabbed the receiver and said, ''Oh Meg, thank God we got ahold of you we were so worried about you we were calling because we just want to know if you're okay and how is your house and what about the windows and are you scared and what about your neighbors and we just want you to tell us that you're fine and then we'll calm down.''

And that's when the phone went dead.

Of course, we did get ahold of Meg a little later and she was okay but a bit scared, the house was okay, and only one window was broken.

When my father was a practicing U.S. Attorney, his specialty was in Indian Land Law. And while I was growing up, it always sounded really cool and politically correct to say that my father was an expert in Indian Land Law . . .

What I didn't explain to my friends was that my dad wasn't exactly on the side of the Indians. The government policy in the Pacific Northwest toward the Native Americans is basically to create a reservation for them, and then later, if they find something valuable on the land, they swoop in and take it back.

And my dad was the guy to swoop in and take it back. There was this one big case that got away from my father during his career, and it involved this Indian family called the "So-Happys." I always loved that name because I thought, *Wow. What a responsibility to live up to.*

Well, the So-Happys had this sacred burial ground and my father was trying to condemn it because the state wanted to build a dam nearby, and it would flood that area. But the So-Happys decided to fight against the building of this dam and for the preservation of their sacred land. They fought valiantly. And in the end, they won.

Well, this was the big case that got away from my father. And sometimes still, many years later, you can find him in the kitchen late at night, with a drink in one hand and the other hand on the counter, looking at the floor, and muttering, "Those damn So-Happys."

As you can imagine, I have very different views on how Native Americans should be treated than my father, and when I was younger, we would get into ethical arguments about it all the time.

For example. There's a creek in Spokane called Hangman Creek, and there's a park next to the creek called Hangman Park. And when we were growing up, we were always saying things like, ''Meet me later down at Hangman Creek,'' or ''Let's go for a hike in Hangman Park,'' and I never really knew why this area was named that. In fact, the name never really registered in my head. And then I became an adult and I read a history of Spokane and I found out how this creek and this park came to be named Hangman.

Apparently in the 1850s, General George Wright came into the Spokane area to try to settle it, and he came up against several Indian tribes who had been living there relatively peacefully for centuries. He found particular opposition with the Spokane tribe and the Palouse tribe, and at one point General Wright asked the six leaders of the Palouse tribe to meet him down by the creek so that they could negotiate some sort of treaty. Well, when the Palouse Indians arrived, General Wright immediately had their horses shot and the Indians hanged. And that's why it's called Hang*man* Creek.

So, one night, in the middle of a particularly tearful—at least on my part—argument with my father, I said, "Well, I'll tell you something! You know why it's called Hang*man* Creek?? I'll tell you why it's called Hang*man* Creek!!" And I proceeded to tell him the story that I just told you.

At the end of my speech there was an awkward pause, and my mother chimed in, "Well, I don't know about that. But I do know that the real estate down at Hangman Creek Golf Course is going through the roof!"

My father is a voracious reader and ever since I can remember there have been books that he's in the middle of strewn all over the house. During the time Mike was sick, he became unusually interested in the Balkans. When you'd walk by his chair, where he sat with his head buried in a book, he might look up at you as you passed by and say something like, "Have you ever heard of Vlad the Impaler?" Or if you were rushing out the door he might grab your arm and say, "If you're interested in the Balkans, might I recommend Rebecca West's travel writings from 1937?"

Okay, Dad. I'll think about that.

Given Mike's situation, and our unusually close quarters, I found this oddly comforting.

Chapter 9
FOOD

NOW, OVER THE COURSE OF THE NINE MONTHS that my parents stayed with me, things started to slowly change around the house. For example, the food.

Where I once had Samuel Adams bottled beer in the refrigerator, that would be drunk and replaced with canned Pabst Blue Ribbon beer.

Or, if I had fresh chunky salsa from Trader Joe's in the refrigerator, that would be eaten and replaced with a can of Del Monte tomato paste that my mother was sure could double as salsa.

Once, when I was out working in my office, my mother came back there and said, "Oh, Julie, I'm sorry to bother you, but I've been through your kitchen, and I can't find your Parmesan cheese." And I said, "Oh, well, actually, I have a chunk of Parmesan in the refrigerator and a grater above the stove." And she said, "What?" And I said again, "I have a chunk of fresh Parmesan in the refrigerator and the grater is in the cabinet above the stove." And she said, shaking her head, "Oh, Julie, you don't have to do all that!"

Even if I used words like "pasta," it was as if I were throwing my big-city ways right into their faces. They'd say, "You mean, noodles?" And if I used a phrase like marinara sauce, it would really blow their minds. So after a few months I was reduced to saying things like, "Hey, how about we have noodles with the red topping for dinner?"

Now, you have to bear in mind that I had spent years in therapy talking about my family and my parents and learning how to do things like, oh . . . set boundaries. But, now here I suddenly was, in this huge situation, with Mike sick and my parents there, and the medical bills mounting. And there was nothing I could do but accept the surreal nightmare that life had become.

Chapter 10
SLEEPING ARRANGEMENTS

WITH MIKE SICK THERE WAS A LOT TO DO.

Mike got radiation five days a week and he got two different kinds of chemo. One chemo he got every three weeks, we called that the Big Chemo. That went into his veins and required him to sit for about four hours with an IV. The other one we called the spinal tap chemo, and that went directly into his spinal column, and that he got every other day.

So just about every day someone was escorting Mike from Hollywood to the UCLA Cancer Center.

There were many other things for us to do, too. Like go to the Social Security office, and stand in line to get the exact right forms to see if Mike could get on Medi-Cal, or figure out how to get a Disabled Parking Pass or go to the pharmacy to get one of Mike's myriad prescriptions filled.

Mike, up until his diagnosis, had been the most private member of our family. He had been a master boundary setter from a very young age. In fact, as a teenager Mike had had a doorbell installed outside his bedroom door. And as an adult, if you said something to Mike like, "Hey, let's go to the movies and have dinner," Mike was apt to respond, "Yes, I can do that on Tuesday between the hours of 6:30 and 9:00, but after 9:00 I have other plans." You really got close to Mike on his terms.

So, for someone like Mike—to be so sick, and in my home, with our parents there—it was a particularly huge invasion of his privacy. So, we all just pretended that my parents were there on this extended visit.

Mike had this habit of asking each doctor or nurse, the first time he encountered them, for their "card" so he could verify their credentials. Then he would quiz them on their educational backgrounds.

I'm not exactly sure why Mike did this, but I think it was just one of the ways he could hold on to a bit of control.

All I knew was that whenever a new medical professional would enter the room, my stomach would tense up because I'd know that at some point Mike would ask them for their card and then ask them about their employment history.

The doctors prescribed Marinol for Mike, which is basically marijuana in pill form. And that's an accepted drug for cancer patients; it helps to keep their pain down and their appetites up. But marijuana in pill form never works nearly as effectively as it does in leaf form.

Fortunately our brother Bill, who lives in Spokane with his wife and kids, was able to get his hands on some real primo stuff.

Bill's always had this talent.

In high school, he'd occasionally sell pot out of the family basement without our parents' knowledge. And my mother was always saying things like, ''Oh, that Bill is so popular! But why do his friends only stay for five minutes?''

Now, for the first few months after Mike's diagnosis, his condition was like a pendulum. Sometimes he would be so sick that he'd have to spend a few nights in the hospital, and sometimes he would feel well enough to go home to his own apartment for the night. But most of the time he stayed at my house, and this is how the sleeping arrangements worked: My parents slept in the guest room, Mike slept in my room, and I slept on the pull-out sofa out back in the office.

And after a few months, the lines started to blur and it became difficult to identify whose house this really was. I think this happened partially because, well, I have a lot of furniture in my house that I inherited from my parents when they moved from the big house to the condo: my coffee table and my end tables and my lamps are all things that I grew up around. With my parents suddenly living with me, and my brother there pretty much all of the time (and my other brothers around all the time), it felt like I was living at home again.

I found myself walking around thinking things like, *When I go to college, I'm gonna get my own dorm room and I'm gonna do whatever I want!* Then I'd remember, *Oh my God, I already went to college.*

It got really noisy and crazy in the house. My brother Bill, who was overwhelmed by Mike's condition, used every vacation day and every extra penny to come down to L.A. again and again. Even Meg was coming over from Japan. And relatives were showing up all the time, and of course Mike had all of his friends around. And instead of the Tchaikovsky that I was hoping to play in the afternoon, we usually had the Irish Rovers blaring.

The feeling at the house was really frenetic.

Chapter 11
THE FELINE RESPONSE

I **THINK IT ALL FINALLY GOT TO BE TOO MUCH** for my orange cat, Gus.

Gus happens to be my most sensitive cat, and I hadn't seen him for a couple of days, and it was raining outside and I was really worried about him. So, I was standing on the porch and I was yelling, "Gus! Gus! Gus!" And then my neighbor came out on his porch and he said, "Hey, Julia. You know, Gus is over here." And I said, "Oh, really?" And he said, "Yeah. You wanna see him?" And I said, "Oh. Yes. I'd love to."

So, I walked out across our yards and into his house and through the living room and down the hallway to the back bedroom and sure enough, there on the back bed was Gus. I said, ''Hi, Gus. How are you?'' And my neighbor said, ''You know, Gus has been spending a lot of time over here. A lot of time. And I believe that Gus thinks he lives here now.''

''Oh,'' I said.

He nodded and added, ''So I eventually went out and got him some food and I made a little bed for him on the floor, but I can shut him out if you want.''

And I said, ''Oh, no! No. I mean if Gus would rather live over here, I guess that would be all right.'' So I turned to Gus and said, ''Would you rather live over here?''

And Gus looked up at me as if to say, ''I'm sorry but the answer is yes.''

I don't know why I ended up giving my cats human names, I think it was because, while all my girlfriends were having babies, I was adopting cats, and I got a little mixed up. Anyway, I also have a cat named Frank. He's black and white and he has the most droll expression. It makes ME laugh every time I look at him. I think Frank's picture should be in the dictionary under ''nonplussed.''

Frank is the cat who never gets ruffled when dogs come around. He is very independent and travels far and wide and most of the people on my street know who Frank is, even if they don't know who I am. In fact, one day I was walking up the block and Frank was walking about fifteen feet in front of me. And a person from a house up the street yelled out, ''Hi Frank!!!!'' really loud. And Frank ran over to this person and got a real quality pet. And this person didn't even know who I was or anything so I just kept walking up the street.

Sometimes I'll walk down my street and I'll see a black and white cat in the distance sitting on someone's porch a block or even two blocks away. And I'll think, *That cat looks just like Frank*. And then I'll get closer and realize it IS Frank.

When my family arrived, there were all kinds of re-adjustments to make for the cats.

I used to have this policy of having the cats in at night, but this immediately went out the window once everyone moved in. I didn't like them running around after dark. Okay, it might seem a little strict for cats, but every night I would make sure the cats were IN before I went to bed. Now, with Rita (my black cat), that was no problem. Rita pretty much stays in all day and if she goes out, it's out only to move about three feet from the house. Plus, Rita seems to need about twenty hours of sleep a day. I have, many times, left my house at eight in the morning, and Rita will be curled up on a chair in the front room. And then I'll come home at six at night and Rita will be in the exact same place in the exact same position on the exact same chair. I always say to Rita, ''Be sure to get your whole twenty hours of sleep today, because you know you're just a wreck and dragging if you don't!''

So, getting Rita in at night just wasn't a problem.

Gus, a voracious eater, who is always hungry, could also be counted on to come home promptly. (Until, of course, he took up new digs next door . . .)

However, Frank was more of a problem. It seemed like every night I would have to stand out on my porch and yell, ''Frank! Frank! Frank!''

One night, a strange man came up my driveway. He said, "What?" And I just looked at him. And he said, "Why do you do that? Why do you call my name out every night. Frank, Frank, Frank! It's driving me crazy!" For a second I thought I should just go with it and pretend that for some reason I was calling his name out at night. But he looked so sincerely distraught, I just couldn't. I had to explain.

In my bedroom there is a door that leads out into my backyard and Rita usually hangs out right outside this door. Before I go to sleep, I always open the door and let Rita in and she'll hop up on the bed and sleep with me. It's always Rita and me on the bed fighting for space. And if you saw how huge Rita is, you would realize it is a true competition.

Well, one night, I was really, really tired. I was so tired, I didn't even turn on the lights in my bedroom, I was just doing your basic catatonic-walk-into-the-bedroom-with-the-lights-out-and-falling-onto-the-bed thing. But Rita was scratching at the door, so I opened it and let her in. She immediately jumped up on the bed and we went to sleep.

Then, about an hour into my sleep I noticed that Rita was being way cuddly. She was purring really loud. Rita is a loud purrer, but this was extra loud purring. And she was licking my nose and face and I kept batting her away. Finally, finally, she settled down and we slept all night.

The next morning I woke up and reached out to pet her and looked over the bed and . . . it wasn't Rita. It was some other cat! Oh my God, it was so horrifying! It was another cat that I'd seen around, a cat that was also black and fat! I went to the door and looked out through the window. There was Rita, sitting right outside the door, looking up at me, MAD AS HELL! I opened it and Rita ran in and the other cat ran out.

Then, whenever I would leave my house, this OTHER black cat would pine away for me from the yard next door. She would look up at me with the most yearning eyes, like she was remembering the wonderful night we had spent together.

Sometimes I would walk to my car and this other black cat would follow me to the car and meow the whole way. I think she was telling me about how we should be together and how could I keep on with such a big fat lazy bitch of a cat like Rita?

Rita turned into a rage machine. Every few days she would venture over to my neighbor's and just beat the crap out of this poor cat. Rita! Who never did anything or went anywhere.

But then Rita found her calling.

Rita became Nurse Rita, because she was constantly with Mike, and he loved it. Since Mike was sleeping in my room most of the time, that meant he was sleeping with Rita, too. When Mike would get home from chemo and need to lie down he would immediately say, "Where's Nurse Rita?" And Rita would run and jump on the bed. (Rita has to get a real real long run going before she can throw her weight up that many feet to the bed, so what would be a small, regular leap for an ordinary-sized cat is a really big deal—a grand gesture—for Rita.)

Then, because Rita was around all the time, either on the bed with Mike, or at her feeding bowl, or walking in between those two places (trying to conserve her energy for the big leap to the bed), everyone got to know her the best.

Sometimes I would get up in the morning and I would find Rita and my mother in some long-drawn-out conversation. Once my mom said to me, "You know what Rita teaches us? That if you are really overweight, it truly is a good idea to wear black because you honestly do look thinner. Rita should be so thankful that she has black fur." So there was Rita, giving us fashion tips.

Chapter 12
PAT IS MAYOR FOR THE DAY

MY BROTHER JIM, WHO, AS YOU KNOW, works for the City of West Hollywood, arranged for me to be honored as "Mayor for the Day." On Halloween. As Pat. I had agreed to do this months before Mike got sick, and months before the movie came out and was a bomb, and months before I never wanted to be Pat again as long as I lived. And months before the public had the exact same feeling about me.

Pat, this character I embodied for a few years on *Saturday Night Live,* is an androgynous being who is chubby to the point where it becomes impossible to distinguish Pat's sexual characteristics (if there are any). Pat has black curly hair and big black glasses. I based the character on a couple of people I used to work with, back when I was an accountant. Oh . . . did I tell you I was an accountant?

When I first came to Hollywood, back in 1982, I had a dream. A dream I'd dreamed since I was a little girl. Oh, it was a familiar fantasy, a tale that's been told a thousand times. I dreamed I would live in Hollywood. I would live in Hollywood and be . . . an accountant. (Maybe I just didn't look at the next career on the list, and see ''actress,'' but that's what I wanted to do . . .)

I went to school at the University of Washington and I got a degree in Economics and European History. And I graduated and headed to Hollywood with my degrees under my arm.

I got a job at Columbia Pictures in the Participation Accounting Department. (I guess I fooled them into believing that all my classes in things like ''Population Economics in India in the Middle Ages'' and ''The Ancient Greek Economy'' had prepared me to calculate percentages of film income in variously complicated configurations.)

While I was at Columbia, I got involved in a special project. The Participation Accounting Department was being moved from New York City to Los Angeles. That meant that several other just-hired accountants and myself were to go to New York and learn what the Big Apple old-time accountants did. And we were to learn what they did just before they lost their jobs. Jobs that many of them had had for more than thirty years. Oh, how neat.

At that time, in N.Y., the Accounting Department employees had desks with adding machines on them. Revenue for each movie was reported on these huge reams of computer paper, which were then identified and hand tallied for each picture according to the contracts for the individual producers. Once you completed writing out your statement (and I mean writing it in pencil), you would take it to the typing department, where ten or so typists sat all day tapping away. They would type it and then you had to proof it against your original.

Finally, a comptroller, a little guy with a big big, more complicated and somehow more reliable adding machine, would check your numbers.

Now, of course, everything is done on computer. But this was way way back in 1982 . . .

So, there was a guy there in the New York office. He had worked at the company for eighteen years and he was in charge of gathering the data for the various films' revenues and inputting them into the system. No one knew exactly how this worked because . . . Wallace (at least that's the name I'll give him here) . . . Wallace was extremely un-communicative, but very sweet. He was beloved by his col-leagues because he was such an eccentric. He was smart, in a very idiot savant kind of way—heavy on the savant. He had developed this computer input system, but he couldn't ex-plain to anyone how it was to be run. I was given a mission. My mission was to get to know Wallace. To sit next to him, befriend him, learn what he did, and gain the knowledge to access his computer system.

I thought, *This will be over in a few weeks. How hard can it be?* What I didn't count on was factoring in Wallace's per-sonality. Wallace wasn't upset that he was losing his job: He was excited about the severance pay. So, we didn't have to worry about that embarrassing complication. What Wallace couldn't do was communicate in any recognizable sort of way. Oh, sure, he used words and even sometimes sen-tences. The problem was, they didn't add up to mean the answer to the question you had just asked.

So, there I was in New York, sitting next to Wallace day in and day out—for six months. Staying at a hotel. The job was all a great mystery. I became a sort of cross between Sherlock Holmes and Dr. Laura Schlessinger. I tried everything. I tried to ask him how he did things. That led to long involved speeches about his wife's spending habits. I tried to watch what he did. That didn't work. I tried to befriend him so I could understand him. This process eventually worked, but it took a long time. Virtually the whole six months.

I finally figured the best way to get into Wallace's head was to just get to know him. I learned everything I could about him. Or at least I thought I did. I heard all about his wife. All about his kids. All about his brother. All about his mother.

For six months, I sat at a desk, in the middle of a big room full of other desks, in a chair right next to Wallace, and I tried as hard as I could to figure out what he did. I accepted that my mission was more psychological than economic. I was here to probe the abyss that was Wallace's mind. And I actually grew quite fond of him.

But Wallace had some personal idiosyncrasies that were annoying.

For example, Wallace always seemed to have stuff coming out of every visible orifice in his body. His eyes were constantly running and he had this drooling problem. Lots of times we would be poring over a computer printout, and drool from Wallace's mouth would come running out and onto the page and into those little holes on the sides, next to the perforated edges. The wetness would ooze onto the paper and slowly fan out as we analyzed the figures. I politely pretended that nothing was happening for—SIX MONTHS. When Wallace had a runny nose, he would roll up tissue and stuff it up his nose and leave it there—two white cones protruding from his nose—and he would think nothing of leaving it there for hours. When he would actually sneeze, his insides would spray out all over his desk— like a cat marking its territory. After a few weeks I would absentmindedly hand him a Kleenex, barely noticing these disruptive eruptions.

Wallace had glasses that were perpetual-glare glasses. You could never see his eyes through his glasses, and it wasn't because they were dark, it was because he always tilted his head up slightly and they would catch and reflect the sparkle of the fluorescent lights and this made his eyes impossible to see. Well, sometimes you could catch a glimpse of them as his head would shoot downward in a sneeze, or on that rare occasion when he would take off his glasses to rub his eyes—which, when he did, would take a good whole five minutes.

So unless you were willing to wait, you would miss your opportunity.

Once I suggested to Wallace that he might be allergic to something and maybe he'd be more comfortable taking an antihistamine. I said, "Wallace. You've got to do something about this." That's when Wallace confessed that he had taken some medicine for it, and it had dried him up, but he was so discombobulated by the lack of mire in his minute-to-minute existence that he immediately stopped it, because of his unusual psychological attachment to his runny eyes and nose.

All right, I'm paraphrasing, he didn't say it like that. If I were to really write what his response was, it would come out something like . . . "Oh, I tried . . . yeah . . . couldn't . . . when did the reports from legal? . . . don't stop mucus . . . what about the Egyptian exchange rate? . . . my nose . . . running." It would be just like that. (And just be thankful I gave you the condensed version.) Apparently, Wallace LIKED having his nose run. I came to believe it was somehow comforting to him.

When our time together was coming to an end, I had to really pressure Wallace to go through his whole desk, to explain every little thing to me. I was going to have to box everything up and send it to L.A., so we really needed to go through it all—together. But every time I suggested we get to this task, Wallace found something else for us to work on.

Finally, it was the last week. I said to Wallace, "Look. I have to clean out your desk. We've been sitting here together for six months. This Saturday I'm going to come in and clean it out. So please, take out all of your personal stuff."

On Saturday I arrived at the office in jeans and a sweat-shirt, ready to do some heavy cleaning. I had boxes stacked up on nearby desks ready to be filled with all of the important paperwork I'd be shipping back to L.A. I started in, purging Wallace's area, and I got to this deep file drawer that didn't have any files in it. Instead it was piled to the top with papers and file folders that had accumulated for years. And at the very bottom, I found some *very* un-work-related material. There, buried beneath years of accounting crap, were dozens and dozens of bondage magazines.

I was stunned. And I didn't know what to do, so I did what anyone would do. I looked through a few of them. They were disgusting.

Now, don't get me wrong. I believe in the right for someone to read these, and therefore the right for someone to publish magazines like this. I mean, I will go to the mat every time for the First Amendment and our right to free speech. But that doesn't mitigate how gross these were.

My big problem now was, what to do with them? I wanted to throw them out, but where? I couldn't very well stick them in the garbage can next to Wallace's desk, so I surreptitiously went around the office and distributed them evenly in each garbage can.

When Wallace came in to the office on Monday, I blushed just to see him. I was so embarrassed for him. I said, "Hi, Wallace. I cleaned out your desk." He didn't look worried, concerned, or at all embarrassed. Could he have not known that they were there? We continued to work together for the final few days as if nothing had happened.

Weirdly, the whole experience made me feel closer to him. My heart went out to him. I had bonded with Wallace through, well, bondage magazines.

Postscript: Months later, long after Wallace had left the company and I was back in Burbank in the L.A. office, I found out that everyone knew about Wallace's predilection for bondage pornography. In fact, at one point, Wallace was even known to read his salacious periodicals at his desk, while he ate lunch. Just sitting back, eating a sandwich, reading the latest issue of *Bondage's Dominatrix Battalion*. And the head of the department had to have a talk with him about reading that material *after hours*. Oh! Wallace!

So, years later, when I had given up my life as an accountant and had decided to become an actress and I was performing at The Groundlings Theater as part of their ensemble, I came up with the character Pat, which is based, in part, on Wallace. Oh, and this other woman that I worked with at Columbia in Los Angeles, who I'll call . . . Muriel.

Every day Muriel, who was rather large, wore either a lime green or fuchsia polyester pantsuit that hugged her like there was no tomorrow. Every single day. It wasn't a great fashion choice for her.

I didn't know Muriel very well, because we worked in different departments, but occasionally I would run into her in the Xerox room. Muriel had a little problem with personal space. What I mean is, if there were only two people waiting in line for the Xerox machine—meaning you and Muriel—she would stand *right* behind you—way too closely. Or if she asked you a question, she would walk right up to your face, until she was just an inch away, and then she'd talk to you in a regular voice, which is at the right decibel level if someone is standing a suitable distance from you.

So, it was basically these two people who I merged together—think of it as the marriage of Wallace and Muriel—

to create Pat. I performed Pat at The Groundlings and it became very popular. And then when I auditioned for Lorne Michaels for a spot on *Saturday Night Live,* I did that character as well and eventually it made its way onto the show and into the homes of people across the country.

The big "joke" of the Pat character is that you can't tell if Pat is a man or a woman and no one is more tired of that joke than me. Even though I love the character of Pat.

Once I was doing these remote radio interviews where you sit in a room and you do one interview every five minutes all across the country. At the station, they asked me if I wanted to do the interview as Julia or Pat, and I said that either was fine. "Okay," they said, "be Pat." So Pat it was. We went on the air and I burst out in typical nasal Pat fashion and said, "Good morning Louisiana! It's Pat!" And the DJ said, "So, Pat . . . We want to know, did you come up with this character yourself? Or did the writers at *Saturday Night Live* come up with it for you?" I said, still in the Pat voice, "Oh, you must be thinking . . ." And then I said in my own voice, "Do you want to talk to me? Julia?" And they said, "Yes! We want to talk to Julia!" And I said, in my own voice, "Hi Louisiana! Good morning!" And they said, "Sooooo, Julia. What are you, a man or a woman?"

I think that, for some people, the line that distinguishes character from actor is very very thin.

So here I was, several years later, and I was getting into the Pat outfit for what I swore would be the VERY last time. And I was traipsing down Santa Monica Boulevard with my brothers Jim and Mike, who was feeling pretty good that day and was wearing his traditional Halloween costume: a priest's habit.

And I had to get up on this stage, and I was just the most halfhearted Pat. I mean, I was just going, ''Eeeew, eeeew.'' And people were walking by and looking up at me and I just know that they were thinking, *That can't possibly be the real person who plays Pat because that would be soooo pathetic.*

I think that my sad display was even too much for Mike, who left halfway through my performance. (Also because he had a date with his radiation therapist, who was meeting him on the corner of Robertson and Santa Monica Boulevard.)

Chapter 13
RADIATION

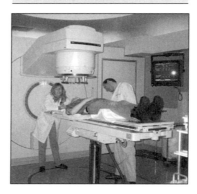

I TRIED TO GO WITH MIKE to all of his radiation appointments.

And we both found it to be very interesting and very high tech. When you get radiation therapy, you must go Monday through Friday, five days a week, for however long. It's like taking antibiotics or something—you can't miss a day.

The very first day takes several hours because they have to figure out exactly where the radiation beams should be sent. Then they usually tattoo that area, so they don't miss when it comes time to zero in with the shot of radiation. These tattoos are nothing elaborate, just a little blue dot on just that spot. Then, after that first visit on day one, the next days are, relatively speaking, easy. You show up, and after waiting anywhere from fifteen minutes to an hour, you're popped into the treatment room and get zapped. That's it. You're free to leave.

The X-ray room is full of equipment and you feel like you're somewhere on the Starship *Enterprise*. When it's the moment of truth, laser beams light up in various colors and zoom in on the exact spot. For Mike, the point of impact happened to be on his head. And, after a few weeks, Mike began to complain, saying that he could feel his skin just starting to burn. His head got real dry and scaly, so we were always putting creams and lotions on it, trying to soothe it for him. But sometimes his head became just too sensitive and he would have a hard time sleeping at night, because even the cotton from the pillowcase would irritate it.

The waiting room was always filled with other radiation patients waiting for their zap. And you had the chance to get to know them because each day you had an appointment at the exact same time like, say, at 11:15, so each day you'd see everyone else who had an appointment in the vicinity of 11:15. Being in the same boat with the same people proved to be comforting.

At first, Mike and I would try to guess their type of cancer, based on how they were wearing the hospital-issue blue-paper cover-up garments, when they emerged from the changing room. We divided Mike's fellow patients into three basic categories: The first group were those who took off their tops, put on a blue-paper smock, and kept their pants on; the second group kept their regular tops on, but their pants or skirts were replaced with blue-paper slacks. Mike was in the third category where he didn't need to change any clothes because all he had to do was take off his hat.

At UCLA they have this sound system in the radiation room and they encourage patients to bring music to listen to. And so, while Mike's brain was being radiated, he usually listened to the Crash Test Dummies or Bach's Unaccompanied Cello Suites.

Mike, being the Sweeney kid most concerned about appearance, was naturally distraught when after the first chemo, he lost all of his hair. But he was eventually able to develop this look for himself. He took to wearing black jeans and a black T-shirt and a black baseball cap.

I gave him this *Reservoir Dogs* T-shirt that he started wearing constantly. And as Mike would come out of the radiation room, he always had this oddly amused expression on his face. And our eyes would meet and then we'd laugh this little laugh like, "How weird is this?"

Mike said that what I was going to get out of his illness was a fabulous doctor husband. And we were always scoping the hallways for the cutest doctors. If a doctor treated Mike and he wasn't handsome enough or single, we'd always ask for a second opinion.

Chapter 14
THE THRESHOLD OF HOPE

WHEN YOU'RE AROUND SOMEONE WHO'S AS SICK as Mike was, you have a couple of urges. One is to be really healthy. I mean, you want to get up and take your vitamins, and exercise, and eat your green leafy vegetables and meditate.

But, on the other hand, you have this equally strong urge to be really *unhealthy*. You want to eat fried foods and drive in fast cars and take up dangerous sports and stuff like that.

One day, I was feeling really stressed out and really down and I became possessed by the latter urge. I really needed a release of some sort, so I decided to do something a little unhealthy and dangerous, and for me that meant to smoke myself a cigarette and buy the new book by the Pope.

Now, as for the Pope, I'm not really a big fan of this Pope (as you can imagine), but I kind of enjoy disagreeing with him on so many topics, so that means that I really have to keep up on what he's saying and writing about. And this was the day that the Pope's new book, *Crossing the Threshold of Hope,* was being released.

Now, as for the cigarette. I really don't *really* smoke— only very, very occasionally—and only when I'm really, really stressed out. And this posed a very specific problem for me now, because my parents are militant nonsmokers.

My father smoked two and a half packs of unfiltered Chesterfields a day until three years ago, and like most former smokers, he absolutely hates smoking. He's always going on about the evils of smoking and I always join in his tirades and agree wholeheartedly.

But that also means that now, if I'm going to indulge in the occasional and for-emergencies-only cigarette, I really have to hide it.

So, on this day I was feeling really down, and I also, not surprisingly, looked just awful. My hair was a disaster and I was wearing these overalls, which is a very bad fashion choice for me.

And I thought, *I can't stand it here anymore! I'm gonna get out of here and smoke me a cigarette and get the Pope's book!* So I got in the car and I headed over to West Hollywood and to Book Soup, which is pretty much my favorite store. I parked and went in, but I couldn't find the Pope's book anywhere. And I suddenly felt really awkward asking for it. (I guess I was just hoping that there would be a big, life-size cardboard cutout of the Pope standing there, a benevolent smile on his face and with his hands open, holding like fifty copies of his own book.)

Finally, I did find his book, and like someone buying pornography, I suddenly felt that I should also get something for on top of it and underneath it. That way, I'd be able to say to the clerk, "You know, I am interested in what the Pope has to say, among so many other things."

So, I started wandering around Book Soup looking for something else to get and my morale was really spiraling downward. No wonder I found myself in the self-help section.

And I just found myself staring up at all the books, when one in particular caught my eye. It was entitled ***The Atheist's Guide to Getting Through the Day: There IS a***

Tomorrow. *Wow,* I thought, *that's interesting that someone would take the time to write* that *book.* Then I thought, *Where the hell's the book called WHAT HAPPENS WHEN YOUR BROTHER HAS CANCER AND YOUR FAMILY MOVES IN WITH YOU?*

And I started feeling worse and worse, and at just this moment—and I hesitate to report this to you because, well, it's embarrassing and also I'm really not into scatological humor in any way, but, at just this moment—I suddenly let out the loudest fart. It was like a foghorn went off in Book Soup. And everyone kind of looked up. I didn't know what I should do. I didn't know whether I should flee the scene or look around like it wasn't me.

Of course, I just stood there frozen, like a deer caught in the headlights. With the Pope's book. God, was I humiliated.

And before I could collect myself, this head came around the bookcase and this guy said, ''Julia? . . . Julia Sweeney?'' I wanted to say, ''You recognized my call?'' but instead I looked up sort of terrified and said, ''Yes?''

And he said, ''Remember me? It's Marshall from The Groundlings Theater?'' I didn't remember Marshall, but I did what I always do in that situation, which is to overcompensate. So I said, ''Marshall! Marshall! Marshall! Wow, it's just so great to see ya, Marshall.'' And he said, ''So, hey, are you still on *Saturday Night Live?*'' And I said, ''No, no. I'm really just . . . not on that show anymore.'' And he said, ''Oh, so, what are you doing now?'' And I said, ''Oh, just, you know, nothing.''

And then he said, ''Oh, hey, how is that Steve? You know, you two are the cutest couple.'' And I said, ''Oh, Steve's doing well. But, you know, we got divorced.'' And then I tried to make my escape, and Marshall came up behind me and he said, ''Oh, hey, how's Mike? Is he still handling the box office at the theater? You know, that Mike Sweeney is so funny.'' And I said, ''Oh, you know, Mike's taking some time off from work right now because . . . he has cancer. Well, nice seeing ya, Marshall.''

And I took my book and I ran up to the register and I paid for it, and you can imagine at this point how much I really, really wanted a cigarette.

So I left Book Soup and I walked up the block to this liquor store and bought a pack of cigarettes. Then I walked back to the car, and I thought, *Okay. There can be no smell of smoke in the car, because I know the next day my whole family will be loading into it to take Mike to chemo.* So, I rolled down all the windows and I started heading east on Sunset, and I lit up my cigarette. And I was holding it outside the driver's window and I was enjoying that cigarette like nobody has ever enjoyed a cigarette.

And I had tears streaming down my face but I was weirdly happy at the same time because I was just so exhilarated to be driving and smoking and to have gotten away from Marshall.

When I got close to my house, I tossed the cigarette out the window. But as I turned down my block, I noticed that I smelled something burning. And then I realized that my car was filling up with smoke. The cigarette must have flown out of the driver's window, and then right back in the rear passenger window. It had landed on my backseat and had . . . ignited it! There was now this little fire smoldering on my backseat.

So, I pulled into the driveway and I jumped out of the car and I opened the back door and I put the fire out and I threw the cigarette out of the car. And I went into the house and my mother greeted me at the doorway and said, ''Oh, I'm glad you're back. I need your car keys. I have to go to the store.''

And I said, ''Oh. Ho, ho . . . The most horrible thing just happened.''

My mother cried, ''What?''

And I said, "Well. I was driving down Sunset Boulevard, and right next to me was this man, this old man . . . in a pickup . . . and he was smoking!"

And my mother said, "Ohhh! Smoking!"

And I loved that her response was so big, like that just might be my whole story.

Then I said, "And he threw his cigarette out of his window and somehow it landed on my backseat and it burned a hole there, which I'm sure you'll see."

And my mother said, "Oh my God, that's the most horrible story I've ever heard! Bob, come out here and hear this awful story!"

So my dad came out into the hallway and I told him the whole story. He said, "Now where was the guy?" And I said, "Right over . . . he was actually on this side . . . and my left passenger window happened to be open. And . . . um."

So, the next morning we all were, in fact, loading into the car to take Mike to chemo. And as we were, my dad leaned down to the grass and then stood up and said, "Look. It's a cigarette."

And I said, "That's it! That's the cigarette the horrible man was smoking!"

And my dad responded, "Wow. Because this cigarette has lipstick on it."

"Oh," I said. "Oh, well. Y'know . . . Sunset Boulevard."

Chapter 15
IN A
LONELY PLACE

AS YOU CAN IMAGINE, things got pretty tense around the house from time to time. And I think that for my mother, my father's drinking and the constant listening to NPR (sometimes she would roll over onto the Walkman in the middle of the night) and, well, sometimes all of it would just drive her nuts.

One day I came in the front door and my mother said, "I need to speak to you privately. Meet me in the hallway." And so, you know, we moved five feet into the hallway. And she said, "Your father is driving me crazy. I am breaking up with him and we are going to separate. But he's not leaving your house, and neither am I." And I said, "Oh!" And she said, "But I do need a new place to sleep because I am not sleeping in there anymore."

At this moment, I'd pretty much had it, and I said, "You know what? No. My policy is that when couples come to stay with me—in my house—they have to remain a couple for the duration of their visit. I do not have enough beds for couples to break up while they visit me!"

But sure enough, for the next few nights, my mother insisted on sleeping on the pull-out sofa in the living room. And during one of those nights, I got up at about three in the morning and went into the kitchen to get a drink of water and I could hear the TV on in the living room. And my mother called out, "Julie. Come in here, I'm watching this incredible movie."

So I did go in there and I saw that she was watching Nicholas Ray's *In a Lonely Place,* which is one of my favorite films noirs. And I said, "Mom, this is an incredible movie, in fact, there's a great exchange just about to come up."

In *In a Lonely Place,* Humphrey Bogart plays this Hollywood writer who's suspected of killing a young hatcheck girl. And Gloria Grahame plays this neighbor of his who ends up providing him an alibi. Well, when Gloria Grahame is at the police station, the officer on duty says to her, "Why were you keeping an eye out for this [Bogart] character?" And she says, "Because I like his face."

Later, when Bogart has her alone at his apartment, he looks into the mirror and says, "How could you like a face like this?" And then he leans into her, and she pulls back and says, "I said I liked it, I didn't say I wanted to kiss it."

We both really enjoyed this and my mother turned to me and said, "If I were her, I would stay away from him, because he obviously has a horrible drinking problem."

And I said, "Well, actually, she might want to stay away from him because, you know, he could have killed that hat-check girl."

But I love that, for my mother, the drinking was the bigger red flag.

After a little while, my father came in and he said, "Oh, I know this movie, this is a great movie." And he sat down on the sofa and we all continued to watch it.

Then Mike came out of his bedroom, and he joined us on the sofa. And at one point, my mom reached over and took Mike's hand and held it. I saw this from the corner of my eye, and I expected Mike to politely let her hold it for a minute, then pull his hand away, because this is something he never would have let her do. But I was surprised that for a long long time, Mike just let her.

We finished watching the movie, and by the time it was over it was about 5:45 in the morning. The sun was just starting to come out and the *L.A. Times* was tripping across the front porch and into the door. We all decided that it was really too late to go back to sleep and that we'd all just stay up and make oatmeal and toast and wait until it was time to take Mike to radiation.

Funny how in the middle of all this, all of these sleepless nights, and the doctor's appointments and noodles with red topping, the most wonderful thing happened.

Chapter 16
CARL

MY GOOD FRIEND DAVID, WHO LIVES IN ASPEN, came down to Los Angeles to visit one time, before the calamity hit my life and home. His brother Carl came along with him, and David introduced us, and Carl and I immediately hit it off. They stayed a few days, and then Carl went back to Pocatello, Idaho, where he was living. Well, we started calling each other and talking on the phone long distance. He was smart. He was funny. And he was cute. You'd think those would be easy qualities to find in a man.

They aren't.

Meeting Carl was a pretty big deal for me because he was the first guy that I was really attracted to since my divorce two years before. I figured we were pretty interested in each other.

Carl's enthusiasm is bow hunting, and even his job is related to this passion. Now, as a virtual vegetarian (at least until my parents arrived) and as a proud volunteering member of PETA, this hobby of his completely disgusted me. But all that woodsy stuff mixed up with *his* personality? Even I had to admit that it was wildly sexy.

Carl and I would talk on the phone and we would get into these big ethical arguments about animal rights. And then I would hang up and go to sleep and dream that he was running after me through the forest—naked, with nothing but a bow and arrow.

I mean, hey, I figure that if you have as dim a view of the future of civilization as I have and believe that it's all going to come crashing down in some sort of post-apocalyptic nightmare, then Carl would be a good choice as a mate.

Well . . .

We continued to talk on the phone, and then, in February, he said he'd like to come down for a visit. Well, this was very, very exciting! A guy who I was romantically interested in was going to visit my cool, girlie bachelorette pad . . .

There was only one problem.

My parents were going to be there.

I kept thinking, *Oh, this is great, I'll have all these candles lit in the living room and I'll have finger food on the coffee table. Carl and I will be snuggled up on the sofa and my mom will walk in, clapping her hands together, and say, "Hey! What's on TV tonight?"*

I mean, how was I going to get my father to clear his 5000-piece puzzle of a map of Sarajevo that he got for his fifty-dollar contribution to NPR off the dining-room table so I could pour some wine and look into Carl's eyes, deeper and deeper than ever before?

Well . . .

What I didn't anticipate was how my parents' presence provided this hotbed of titillation the likes of which I had never experienced before.

You see, my parents, well, they know I'm not a virgin. I mean, I was married for five years. But, by the same token, they're not really going to condone me starting up a sexual relationship with someone right under their noses. On the other hand, I am an adult and this is my house, so it was kind of a tricky situation.

It meant that Carl and I had to sneak around.

And I haven't had to sneak around with a guy for about sixteen years and, you know, I forgot. I forgot how exciting that is.

Carl slept on the pull-out sofa in the office out back and I slept out on the sofa in the living room and we would spend time with the family and then at night I would go out and say "good night" to Carl, for, you know, about an hour.

We found ourselves playing footsie underneath the dining-room table, and my mother was suddenly making all these traditional meals and saying things like, "You two be sure to be home at six, I'm making meat loaf!"

I felt like a Catholic schoolgirl again and I was saying things like, "Oh, my parents are so weird. Let's go make out in the garage."

One day, Carl and I went to Will Rogers State Park for a hike, and when we got home in the late afternoon, there was no one else there. And that was incredibly unusual, I mean, there was always someone at the house.

We walked in and I said, "Oh my God, Carl. No one's home! Get in the bedroom. Take off your clothes. Now!" And Carl said, "Oh, okay. But I just noticed that your garbage cans are empty down on the curb. Do you want me to move them up to the side of the house first?" And I said, "No, we don't know how much time we have. Get in the bedroom. Take off your clothes. Now!" So he did and I did and *we did*.

Then after a while we came back out to the living room and Carl looked out the front window and he said, "Julia, your garbage cans. They've been moved up to the side of the house." And I said, "Really?" And he said, "Yeah. Who would have done that?" And I said, "I don't know. I don't think any of my neighbors would do that. I mean, look. All of their garbage cans are still down on the curb." And Carl said, "You don't think that your parents came back here, and heard us, and were embarrassed and decided to leave, but before they left, they put the garbage cans up by the side of the house?" And I said, "No. I don't think so. My parents are so naive and plus we weren't very loud, or at least I don't think we were . . ."

The next day the exact same thing happened. We got back in the afternoon, we walked in, and there was nobody there. And I said, "Oh, Carl. I just wish I knew how much time we have." And Carl said, "Me too."

At just that moment the phone rang and it was my father. He said, "Julie, this is Dad. Listen, um, your mother and I are in Santa Monica and we're heading home. And we just wanted you to know that you should expect us in about forty-five minutes."

Chapter 17
I LOVE MY SHUNT

WELL, WE WERE ALL CONTINUING TO HELP MIKE and take him out to UCLA, for all of his different therapies, and he was doing very well, with the exception of the spinal tap chemos. Mike had gotten so many spinal taps that scar tissue had built up along his spinal column and they couldn't access it anymore.

One day, we were at the medical center, and Mike was in the examination room, up on the table. My brother Jim was there, and my mom, and my dad, who was reading a 30,000-word article in *The New Yorker* all about the plague in India, you know, as a diversion. The doctor came in and he said, "Mike, this is what I suggest. I think that we should put a shunt—which is a plastic opening—into your forehead so that we can put the chemo directly into your cranial fluid.''

Mike said, ''Listen, Doc, if you think you're gonna put a faucet into my forehead, you may as well give me a lobotomy at the same time.''

Then there was this awkward pause and my mother chimed in and said, ''Oh, Mike. I don't think it's like a faucet. I think it's more like a . . . a spigot.''

I think even the doctor was embarrassed. He said, ''Well, Mike, let me tell you something. My patients who have the shunts, well, they, they LOVE them.'' And Mike said, ''They do, do they? Then by all means give me a shunt.''

So Mike got a shunt. And after that his refrain became, ''I love my shunt!'' Every time the doctor came into the examination room, he'd say, ''Hi, Mike. How're you doing?'' And Mike would say, ''I'm not doing too well, Doc, but I'll tell you one thing. I love my shunt!''

And to just show you how surreal things were getting, at night, the whole family would watch shows like *ER* and *Chicago Hope* and whenever anyone would come into the emergency room Mike would yell out, ''Give 'em a shunt! They need something to love!''

Chapter 18
I KNOW WHERE I'M GOING

I HAVE A FRIEND, RICHARD, who can do something quite amazing. He can make VCRs record shows at times that you preset into your machine! And not only that, he can make the clock tell the right time! Imagine! And he visited me from N.Y., long before everyone had moved in.

I got him to preset my VCR to record *The Larry Sanders Show* at 3:00 A.M. on Wednesday mornings. I was so excited.

But two problems instantly arose.

One was that *The Larry Sanders Show* immediately changed to another time, and forget it if you think I was going to be able to learn how to change the time myself without attending some sort of special class.

And secondly, for some strange reason, when the VCR popped on, the TV popped on too, and at the volume level it had been on when the TV had been turned off.

So that meant that every Wednesday morning at 3:00 A.M. the TV came on. Now, I usually remembered to turn the volume down on Tuesday nights so that it wasn't so noisy when the TV came on all by itself. I remembered because I put a Post-it on the remote to remind myself.

If you think that doing this is a lot more complicated than finding out how to just, oh, say, stop the machine from turning on in the first place, then you don't understand that oft-held feminine quality to instinctively accommodate rather than to solve.

It took me a whole week after we watched *In a Lonely Place* to realize that my mother hadn't been sitting up restless, watching TV, when she'd summoned me from the kitchen to watch it with her. That she had probably been woken up by the blaring television. And that instead of turning off the television, she just started watching whatever was on. (Which sort of tips you off to from where, on the family tree, I inherited this quality myself.) But then she actually got involved in the show, and I really love her for that quality—her ability to just give herself up to something, even if it is three o'clock in the morning.

That's what life was like then, all accommodation and no solving. Because there wasn't a solution to the big things, and it made us not even try to solve the littler things.

My friend Richard could do something else that was really really great. Even though he lived in New York, he would send me videos of movies to watch. Videos he would make from his laser disc player.

This is how he came to send me *I Know Where I'm Going*.

It's a 1945 English movie by Michael Powell and Emeric Pressburger. Basically, it's about a young woman who is engaged to a wealthy older man and she's traveling by train to the north of Scotland to go off to an island to meet up with him and marry him there. I won't ruin it for you, but let me just say, she gets a little sidetracked.

The theme song for *I Know Where I'm Going* is sung by one of those forties soprano vibratos and the lyrics are: "I know where I'm going, and I know who's going with me. I know who I love, but the dear knows who I'll marry."

We all watched this movie, over and over. We loved it. For some strange reason, we identified with it. And naturally, the theme song started getting stuck in all of our heads. We'd find ourselves humming it all the time, and then singing it. And sometimes we'd find ourselves humming it at the hospital, and eventually we started to use it as a homing device to find each other. You'd be walking by the gift shop and you would hear this familiar tune, and you would look in and there'd be one of us Sweeneys, buying some Life Savers. For the first time, I felt like we were a tribe. And one with our own not-completely-logical theme song.

One night, as we were watching the movie, my mother came in from the kitchen and said, ''Who wants some Mary Magdalene Tarts?'' And I said, ''What?'' And she said, ''Remember at *Nunsense,* they gave out these cookbooks, and there was a recipe for Mary Magdalene Tarts, and I just made some.''

That's pretty damn funny, Mary Magdalene Tarts. I was probably too tough on that show. And besides, they tasted great.

Chapter 19
SYMPATHY CANCER

ONE TIME WHILE MIKE WAS GETTING CHEMO, just to make conversation with one of the nurses, I said, "Hey, do you know of any gynecologists in town because I've just moved out here from New York and I need to get started with someone new." And she said, "Oh, yes," she knew this wonderful gynecologist and she wrote down his name and number and I put it in my back pocket.

And when I got home, instead of just filing the number away, because it was really months before I needed to make my annual exam, I decided to call and make an appointment.

And I went in. And I was examined. And about a week later I was in my office and I got a call from my doctor and he said, ''Julia, we got the test results back. And I'm sorry, but it appears that you have cancer.'' And I said, ''What!?'' And he said, ''Yes. You have cervical cancer and it's spread to your uterus and your fallopian tubes and I recommend that you get a hysterectomy right away.'' And I said, ''But, this is impossible! You know, my brother has cancer.'' And he said, ''Oh, really. What kind?'' And I said, ''Lymphoma.'' And he said, ''Oh, that's completely unrelated.'' And I said, ''Well, I know it's unrelated. I'm just saying this is just horrible timing. I mean, couldn't this wait?'' Obviously it couldn't.

And I hung up and I looked back from my office into the back of the house and I could see through the windows my mother in the kitchen cooking, and my father hovered over the dining-room table, and Mike in my bedroom. And as I walked across the backyard I actually considered not telling them. But I didn't know how I was going to hide having a hysterectomy.

So. I went into the house and I told everybody and of course, you know, they were devastated, and Mike immediately said, ''Oh, you just couldn't stand it, could you? I bet it was hard for you, being an actress, with me in the cancer spotlight all the time!'' And then later he said, ''Jules, you just got a little sympathy cancer.''

Between Mike and me that was really no joke. We really felt like I did have sympathy cancer.

Well there I was having to lose my reproductive organs. And, you know, I always figured I'd have a child someday, but I had never chosen to up until this time and now it looked like that was going to be impossible. I guess I always thought of my reproductive organs like this great shiny bike that I had in the garage that I was totally going to ride someday. But I never had taken the opportunity to ride it yet, and now someone was stealing my bike.

On the other hand, if you have to get cancer you actually have an advantage in having cancer of a reproductive organ. Because you can simply take it out. I mean, it's not like having cancer of the liver or the lungs, where you need that organ to continue daily existence. With a reproductive organ, you simply remove it.

So this led me to thinking, what if you got cancer of the fat? Then you'd have to have this emergency liposuction. And my doctor told me that some people actually do get cancer of the fat.

Chapter 20
DR. FU

WELL, MY DOCTOR TOLD ME TO CALL the Cedars Sinai Comprehensive Cancer Center to make an appointment. And when I did, the receptionist was a little less than accommodating. She said, "Oh, yes. I have your name here. Miss Weenie." I said, "No, that's Sweeney." And she said, "Yes, Miss Weenie." And I said, "No, that's Sweeney." And she said, "That's a weird name. Weenie." And I said, "No, it's not! 'Cause it's Sweeney!" And she said, "Oh, well. I can't make an appointment for you right now because it turns out that your cancer is a very rare type of cervical cancer and they've sent all of your slides to the

UCLA Pathology Department where they are studying that type of cancer there.''

And I said, ''Oh. Wow. Well, is there some way we could get these slides back, so I could make an appointment so I could, you know, try to get rid of this cancer?'' And she said, ''Well, the courier service is taking a really long time.'' And she really didn't know when they could get the slides back. So then I said, ''Well certainly there's something we could do to help expedite this process.'' And then she said, ''Well, I suppose if you'd like to pick them up?'' And I was thinking, *I bet she's never asked anyone to pick up their own slides ever.* But I said, ''Well, coincidentally, I will be at the UCLA Cancer Center tomorrow and I suppose I could just hop over to Pathology and pick up my slides.'' And without seeming to blink an eye or note the irony in that statement, she agreed. And the next day, while Mike was in the chemo lounge I set about to get my slides.

Well. The Pathology Building at UCLA is this big eight-story building and it's not set up to have any regular person go into it. And there's no reception area, there's no directory of doctors, there's no nothing. And I went in and I found myself walking through these doors that were marked GREENS ONLY, NO PUBLIC ADMITTANCE. And, in fact, the people were wearing green lab wear and masks and the hallways were lined with what looked to me like Tupperwares filled with lungs. And I was just trying to get someone to recognize me as an alien and finally this woman did.

And I said, "Yes. My name is Julia Sweeney and I'm looking for my slides." And she said, "Oh. What research project are you working on?" And I said, "Oh, no research project. They're slides of me. They're my slides." And she said, "Oh. Nobody picks up their own slides." I said, "Yeah, that's what I thought." And she looked at this computer program and she said, "Your slides are with a Dr. Yao Fu and he's up on the eighth floor."

Well, I went up to the eighth floor and I found Dr. Fu's office door and I opened it. And it was like something out of a movie set. There were books piled high to the ceiling and there was a Xerox machine next to a filing cabinet next to a microscope and peering over his microscope was Dr. Fu.

And I said, "Hello, Dr. Fu? My name is Julia Sweeney and I'm looking for my slides." And he said, "Oh. What research project are you working on?" I said, "No research project. They're slides of me." And he said, "Oh. Nobody picks up their own slides." And I said, "I know." And he said, "Wait a minute, you mean to tell me that you have this cancer?" And I said, "Yes." And he said, "Oh my goodness. This is incredible, you know, I have been studying this very rare kind of cervical cancer here at UCLA for the last twenty years, and I've never actually met someone who had the cancer.''

And I said, ''Oh, Dr. Fu, here I am.'' And he said, ''Wow, you know, I just read these profiles, and look at these slides. You know, this is a very rare type of cervical cancer, there've only been fifty diagnosed cases so far, and none of them have died.''

And I said, ''Oh. I feel so lucky.'' Then he said, ''Wow, this is very exciting. Do you mind if I take you out for a cup of coffee?'' And I said, ''No, I don't mind.''

And so we went and got coffee and he told me all about his research and theories and I told him all about me. And at one point he took this torn AT&T envelope out of his back pocket and he put it on the table and he drew my reproductive organs and he kind of explained to me what they were going to do and then he said, ''Are you sad about losing your fertility?'' Only he said, ''Fertirity.'' And I said, ''Yes. I am sad about it. But, you know, I'd rather live.'' And he said, ''Yes. Living is better.''

And so we walked back to his office and on the way he even squeezed my arm and said what a wonderful day this was. And it was true, it did turn out to be the most delightful afternoon.

So I don't know . . . I figure, if I have to be the kind of girl that they ask to pick up her own slides, when they would never ask anyone else to pick up their own slides, and if I happen to be the kind of girl who they always forget at Starbucks, then at least I'm the kind of girl who gets to meet people like Dr. Fu.

Chapter 21
HOUSE GUEST

ONE NIGHT I WENT TO THE LATE SHOW of the movie *House Guest*. My good friend Phil Hartman was in it and I was going to see him the next week, and I wanted to be able to say something really nice about his latest film.

When I came home, I was in a sour mood because, well . . . I had not exactly accomplished my task. Let me put it this way: If I had to choose an example of Phil's best work this wouldn't be it. And, well, maybe also because I had cancer, and my brother had cancer, and my parents were living with me—okay, maybe that also contributed to my depressed feeling.

I walked in the front door and Mike was lying on the sofa, and he just didn't look very good. He had his arms crossed over his chest, and his eyes were looking up to the ceiling, and his jaw was slack. I said, ''Mike, how're ya doin'?'' And Mike said, ''Hey, I'm feeling pretty good today.''

''That's great,'' I said, and I headed for the kitchen and my mother intercepted me and she said, ''Oh! How was *House Guest?* I love that Sinbad, I see him on TV and your TV isn't working because the cable is out of sync with the channels on the TV and I don't know how to fix it and I want to because I have a video I want to watch but I can't because I'm making soup in the kitchen but the soup is boiling over and your father could finish it, but he can't because he's been drinking.''

So I headed into the kitchen and my father said, ''Hey, how was *House Guest?*'' And I said, ''Fine.'' And he said, ''That Phil Hartman is hilarious.'' And I said, ''Yes, he is . . .'' And then my mother came in and said, ''You're out of cat food. There's no cat food.'' And I noticed that Frank and Rita were underfoot and adding to the noise and going ''Meow, meow, meow.''

I must stop at this point to tell you that, at this moment, every available audio device in my house was on: the radio in the kitchen, the stereo in the dining room, the TV in the living room. And there's not a lot of space in between those places.

And now the cats were going "Meaow! Meaow!" And my mother said, "I would have gotten some cat food, but I don't know what kind they like and you get mad when I get the wrong thing." So I said, "Fine, I'll go to the store."

So I went to my nearby grocery store, Pavillions. And they were having this big sale on Friskies, like three for eighty-nine cents. So I decided to get a bunch. And . . . You know, when you're in the grocery store at midnight, on a Friday night, buying fifteen dollars' worth of cat food, and you're a single woman in her mid-thirties . . . well, that's a special feeling . . .

I got home and I found that while I'd been gone, my father had decided to put dry food into the cat food bowls. But it was the dry food my cats hate. And so I picked it up to throw it out, and my dad grabbed the other side of the bowl and said, "Don't throw it out, we can save it in the Tupperware."

And I saw that he had a little Tupperware bowl out.

And I said, "No, this is the kind they hate, I'm just going to throw it out."

And he said, ''No, we shouldn't waste it, let's save it in the Tupperware.''

And I said, ''No, let's just throw caution to the wind and throw it out.''

And he said, ''But I got out the Tupperware.''

And I said, ''Even if I were going to save it I wouldn't save it in the Tupperware!''

And we went back and forth, and of course the bowl flew into the air, and cat food went everywhere, including into the soup that was boiling over on the stove.

Immediately the phone rang. It was my sister Meg, calling from Japan. And she was very upset. She said, ''Hi. Thank God you picked up. Mom and Dad sent me a letter demanding that I pay them the forty-eight dollars that I charged onto their Visa for the subscriptions to *National Geographic* that I gave everybody for Christmas. And they want me to pay them—before they get their bill! So I just wrote them a check for a hundred dollars, and I'm putting a note in with it that says, 'I don't want to have any more dealings with you!' ''

And I'm thinking, *You already live in Japan! How much less can you have to do with them?* And then I just loved that I not only had to be one of the recipients of the gift of the *National Geographic* subscription, but I also got to hear about all the trauma and the subterfuge surrounding the paying for it.

So while I was on the phone with Meg, my mom came up and just started talking, even though I was on the phone, which is something she does, and she said, "Have you heard of a place called the House of Blues? Everybody's talking about the House of Blues. I love blues. I just love blues and gospel. That's because I love Gershwin."

Now, ten years ago, if she had said that, I would have pointed out that Gershwin was not gospel, but that they did share the same first letter. But now, when my mother says things like that, I just say, "Uh-huh."

Chapter 22
INTERNATIONAL HOUSE OF CANCER

MY PARENTS HAVE THESE FRIENDS, THE PASBYS, who live in Palm Springs and they're really good old friends of theirs. They just love them. In fact, Bob Pasby was the best man at their wedding. And sometimes they go off to Palm Springs and visit the Pasbys. To give you an idea of Bob Pasby's personality, let me tell you a little story. Once when he and his wife came to L.A. to visit us, we all went out to breakfast at ten in the morning at Canter's Deli. Bob Pasby ordered a boilermaker, and I looked at him and he said with a wink, "Just trying to level the playing field."

So, my parents decided to go off and visit their friends the Pasbys and that left Mike and me at home alone. And both of us having cancer. Well, we immediately started answering the phone, "House of cancer!" And we seriously considered putting a sign out front that said INTERNATIONAL HOUSE OF CANCER.

If anything wasn't working, or a houseplant was a little droopy, or even if a tree out front was a little sad-looking, we'd say, "Maybe the tree has cancer."

And my black cat, Rita, she started to lose the hair on her back and on her sides. And we started thinking, *Oh no! Now Rita has cancer!* But we took Rita to the vet and the vet assured us that Rita did not have cancer, although he couldn't explain why she was losing her hair.

A few weeks before, Mike had had a port put into his abdomen so that we could pump nourishment directly into his stomach, because he was having such a hard time digesting food. And it was working pretty well. But during this time we were alone together, he suddenly started to have a really bad reaction to it.

One night he started throwing up and throwing up and it didn't seem like there was any end in sight. And Mike was really reluctant to go to the hospital. For him it just meant losing control, so he would always wait until the very last moment before he would go. Finally, at three in the morning, when there had been no letup of his vomiting, we both agreed that he just had to go to the emergency room.

Chapter 23
THE LONG, LONG DRIVE

MIKE AND I GOT INTO THE CAR TO MAKE THAT LONG, long drive down Beverly Boulevard, to Santa Monica Boulevard, to Wilshire Boulevard, to Westwood, to the UCLA Cancer Center. When you're driving at that time in Los Angeles, there is no one else on the road, and L.A. really becomes the desert it always was meant to be.

Mike was in the passenger seat and he was leaning up against the car door trying not to throw up in the car. And he was wearing his *Reservoir Dogs* T-shirt, which was by then worn thin and stained.

I was driving the car thinking, *Now I have cancer too*. At one point Michael said, "What did I do to deserve this?" That was so unusual, I mean, Mike never asked why. I said, "Mike, no one would deserve this. No one." And Mike said, "Yeah, even Christ only suffered for a day."

We got to the emergency room and they could see that Mike was really dehydrated. They wanted to get a saline solution into him right away, but the veins in his arms were all exhausted and so they were trying to get a needle in up over his ear. And he was continuing to throw up and I was standing in the doorway looking in on this. And, to just show you what a wonderfully dark sense of humor Mike had, in even the most horrific of circumstances, he turned to me and said, "I guess it's not so funny now that you have cancer too, huh?" And I said, "Yeah, Mike. 'Cause normally I'd be laughing my ass off."

An emergency room is a strange place to be at three in the morning. And I guess I expected it to be more like *ER* or something. But it was weirdly quiet. The room isn't really that big and the little rooms that the patients were in were pretty much empty. Mike and I sat in one room while the saline solution dripped into him. And we listened to the man next door. He was a big overweight man who was clearly mentally handicapped. He didn't seem to be homeless, but he sounded like he was just an inch away from being there.

He kept complaining to the emergency-room nurse about his diabetes and the eczema on his legs. He talked compulsively and nonstop all about his dog and his dog's illnesses. He talked about how his hands were swelling, his ears were getting bigger, and they hurt. He had a pain, and every time he was asked about it, it had traveled to another place. To his leg. To his arm. Now it was in his chest. When the doctor came in, the man said, "I'm here for my heart attack." Like it was a hair appointment.

A hospital provides nonstop entertainment. There are the brave people, the tragic people, the crazy people.

As the saline solution dripped into Mike's arm, we just sat and stared at the wall we shared with the crazy man we couldn't see. It was like watching a television show with a screen the size of the whole wall, but with the picture off. A few months before, Mike and I would have been suppressing our laughter. But by now, we just looked at each other, smiled weakly, and shook our heads occasionally. These bizarre scenes had now become our norm. Everything seemed so incredibly regular.

At eight o'clock in the morning, I got up and went to a pay phone and called over to Cedars Sinai, because they needed to get some insurance information straight before my impending surgery. It felt ghostly, standing in the emergency-room hallway, waiting for Mike to get discharged, on the pay phone with another hospital, the hospital that would soon be mine.

Finally they determined that Mike was adequately hydrated and we went home. And my parents returned, and Mike seemed to get a bit better.

Then he got worse. And worse.

One night, Mike just insisted that he stay at his own apartment. He was tired of staying with me and I could see why. His apartment reminded him of himself. And he was starting to forget himself and he needed the reminding.

But he had to have the feeding machine with him, and it was a bit of a production. We moved it over there and Dad and I set it up so it could drip and ooze into him while he sat or lay on the sofa. He said he could sleep there fine, and that way he could watch TV if he woke up in the middle of the night.

But we didn't like the idea of him being totally alone. So, we decided to alternate staying with him; sometimes Mom and Dad would stay over. Then I would stay over. Then Jim would stay over. And when Bill was in town, he would stay over.

Mike had a water bed. He'd always had one. He couldn't understand why anyone wouldn't have one. It was like being on a boat to him, and he loved that. But I'd never really slept on one before, and since Mike was confined to the sofa, I finally got my chance to get that womblike feeling that Mike had raved about for so many years.

We kept the door between the bedroom and living room open so we could talk. Mike and I talked almost all night long through the open door. We remembered *Gilligan's Island* episodes we loved. We sang the song. Mike was coughing a lot and he was starting to have a hard time talking. I believed that the slur in his speech was from the painkillers, and I'd often argue with him that I thought he was taking too many. But my ''know-it-all'' attitude was wrong. Something more sinister was going on for Mike—something much more terrible than taking too many drugs. The cancer was still growing. Despite the chemo, the radiation, despite everything.

We talked until I could hear that Mike had nodded off and all I could hear was the ticking click of the feeding contraption.

This was my old apartment. The one Mike had sort of inherited from me, where I'd lived for seven years. It had been my first apartment all to myself, and then later I had shared it with Steve after we were married. Our whole marriage, basically, was spent in this apartment.

And so I was lying there, looking at the ceiling, seeing the paint that was still there after nine years, when I had first moved in and had painted the bedroom a very girlish pink. Mike had painted white over the top of it, but parts of the old paint still peeked through at the corners near the window.

This room was so familiar and so foreign, it sent shivers down my spine. But the water bed lulled me into a dreamy state, morphing the past and present.

Chapter 24
MIKE GETS SICKER

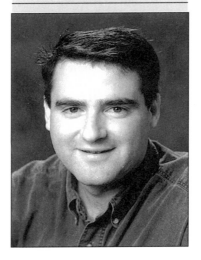

I GUESS IT'S HUMAN NATURE TO WANT TO FIND even the smallest reason for the person to be responsible for their own misfortune, but in the end, sometimes really shitty things happen to innocent people, and there's not a damn thing that can be done about it.

The new discoveries of Mike's elusive cancer opened a flood of sadness for me. I couldn't sleep anymore. I would close my eyes and only see Mike's now-small frame in the hospital bed. He seemed like a wounded bird lying there, his big eyes just looking up at you. And his smile was so big because his face had become so small. It was hard to believe that this was the same brother that used to put me into a headlock on the front lawn and hold me down until I cried uncle.

I couldn't cry deeply enough. Hard enough. Memories of our life together were constantly hemorrhaging into my head. I know that's a strong image, but that's what they felt like, a hemorrhage. Besides our familial relationship with all the usual memories, he had been the center of my life since August in a very big way. I was completely unprepared emotionally for him to die.

The hospital instructed us to have Mike sign Power of Attorney forms while he still could, to make a will, to get his banking taken care of, etc.

I drove out to Mike's credit union to get the forms to have a joint account created. I was crying so hard I missed the exit off the freeway and it took me thirty minutes to get turned around again. I kept taking wrong turns and forgetting where to park, going through wrong doors, leaving the deposit slips in the car, oh God, it was awful. When I finally got back to the hospital, Mike signed the papers, putting Jim and me in charge of making any major medical decisions. Then Mike signed his bank account over to me and my mother cried. When it was all over, we just sat there, like, okay, now what? Is this when he dies?

We were all just silent. What do you say in a situation like that? And then Mike sat up in bed with what seemed like renewed vigor. He smiled and suggested we all watch the O. J. Simpson trial. He said he was looking forward to the next witness, who was a bartender at the restaurant where Nicole ate the night of her death. (Apparently, according to Mike, Nicole had eaten fusilli with marinara sauce on the night of her murder.) So, we all pulled up chairs and watched the O.J. trial for the rest of the afternoon.

Then Mike started feeling a whole LOT better. He challenged me and Dad to a game of Scrabble. Mike won easily with a triple word bonus on the word "exit."

Chapter 25
HEAVEN IS AN INSTANT

BUT MIKE'S GOOD DAYS BECAME FEW AND FAR BETWEEN, and his condition worsened even more. A day was a triumph if he was able to eat a meager breakfast.

It was around this time that the family made this non-verbal shift in our hopes. And we stopped praying for Mike to get better and started to pray for an end to his suffering.

Then Mom started talking about Mike going to heaven.

Heaven. That word. It reminded me of when I was in high school and in junior year I was taught religion class by Father Fitterer.

Father Fitterer was a Jesuit, a scholar, and a thinker. And he was the first person to introduce me to any sort of existential-like ideas.

One day in our religion class, he said, "Perhaps heaven is an instant. If there's no time after death, perhaps heaven is just that light at the end of the tunnel, that great moment of awareness, and it happens just like that." And he snapped his fingers. "Heaven is an instant."

While this concept might sound really simple to you and me now, at the time it was mind-blowing for me, and I could hardly wait to share it with someone. I wanted to tell my mother.

I raced home after school, but I couldn't find my mom anywhere. I finally found her in the back bathroom, Cometing out the tub.

"Mom!" I said. "Father Fitterer said that heaven is an instant."

And she stood up and she said, "What?"

And I said, "Yeah, Father Fitterer said that, you know, if there's no time after death, maybe heaven's just that light at the end of the tunnel. And it's just like that, heaven is an instant."

And then my mother, with the Comet in one hand, took the other and slapped me across the cheek. And I could never understand why she would have that reaction. But, maybe you don't walk into the bathroom of a Catholic mother of five who's Cometing out the tub and tell her that heaven is an instant.

It was really important for my parents that Mike receive last rites. I was actually opposed to this because I didn't want to send a signal to Mike that we didn't think he was going to make it. But my parents' wishes prevailed, and one afternoon when I was spending time alone with Mike in the hospital and he was actually having a pretty good day and we were playing Scrabble, in came Father Sullivan, in his Roman collar, clearly there to give Mike last rites. And Mike, being Mike, immediately asked him for his card and started quizzing him about his credentials.

Father Sullivan said, "Mike, you're just gonna have to take it on faith this time." And so there, over the Scrabble board, Mike received the last rites.

After Father Sullivan left, Mike turned to me and said, "Mom and Dad sent him." And I said, "Oh, I know. I'm sorry." And Mike said, "No, actually, that was pretty cool."

Mike continued to decline and pretty soon his organs started to go one by one. But he just kept on ticking and the doctor said that he would. He said he had the heart and lungs of a thirty-one-year-old and he was just going to keep on ticking for a while. But soon even the doctors couldn't explain why Mike was still alive and eventually one doctor suggested that maybe it was just psychological at this point. Maybe Mike just wasn't emotionally ready to go.

So, they sent this therapist in to talk to Mike. And she sat down next to his hospital bed and said, "Mike, I want you to visualize that you're on a trampoline right now. Imagine yourself going up and down and up and down and really feel yourself going up and down. And now I want you to imagine just jumping off to the side a little bit."

Jim was with Mike when he died a few hours later. He, and some of Mike's closest friends, had put buckets of water at the sides of the bed and they put his hands in it and they said to him, "Mike, you're in a boat. We're ferrying you." And they even picked up the mattress by the edges and swayed it gently back and forth. It was like a water-bed ferry boat, and Mike loved water and boats. He loved the ocean, and he loved traveling to places like Hawaii. And then he drew his final breath.

So that's how Mike died. Being ferried across by his friends.

I wished I'd been there. Mom and Dad and I were actually at home when it happened. We had been on a ''death watch'' for so many days that you had to give up on the idea of planning to be there with him at the final moment. It was either going to happen that way or not.

It's funny how that works. A woman who worked at The Groundlings, and whom Mike only knew casually, happened to come by to visit him just at the moment of his death. I still see her around occasionally, and we sometimes share awkward glances. But to me, it's wonderful that she was there. And my Aunt Bonnie and Uncle Tom walked in just minutes after Mike died. They live in Seattle and were very, very close to Mike. Tom had had a feeling that morning that they should get on a plane and fly to L.A. So they left their respective jobs and just got on a plane, without telling anyone their plans. They took a cab right from the airport to the hospital, and when they arrived, everyone was still standing around him, in shock, in reverie, in peace, taking it all in.

I'm so glad Mike had such a beautiful death. When you think of all the horrible deaths there are, that people have had, Mike's seemed to be one of the most pleasant at the very end. And since death is a birth too, I hope he felt his delivery was untraumatic and somehow rejuvenating, even if the long journey leading up to it was hellish.

And I hope that for Mike, finally giving up all control meant that he ultimately gained some.

Chapter 26
HYSTERECTOMY

THREE DAYS AFTER MIKE PASSED AWAY I was scheduled for my hysterectomy.

I really wanted my parents to go back home. I just figured that we were all so sick of being around people who were sick. I found myself saying the strangest things like, "My friends who've had hysterectomies didn't have to have their parents stay with them. They got to have their hysterectomies on their own!" But my parents insisted on staying and so they did.

I have to say, I was so whacked out from Mike dying that I barely thought about my own impending surgery. In a way, it was a blessing. I am sure I would have been very insecure and psychologically overwrought if I were just dealing with my own cancer, out of the shadow of Mike's. But somehow, my cancer seemed like an afterthought, an embarrassment really. And everyone was so exhausted and unraveled from Mike that I felt like someone complaining about their cough at a funeral.

I just wanted to get it over with.

I had two strong feelings about the procedure I was about to undergo. I'll admit, the first was cosmetic. Every time I got out of the shower, I would look at my stomach and I would try to memorize that image. My pre-hysterectomied scarless abdomen. I would just stand there as the steam moved around the bathroom, and the mirror slowly came to reflect my hazy form. Then I would wipe a part of the mirror with my hand, the part that revealed my tummy, and just stare at its smoothness.

I mean, don't get me wrong—my stomach has never been my strong point and it's no tragedy to have a scar there. In fact, I subscribe to the belief that scars are badges of honor. No, for me, the stomach-staring phase I went through was more about the permanent change of it. I re-membered when my mother told me I was going to grow pubic hair, and I was so shocked and bewildered that I would stare at my nether region in the mirror and imagine how it

would be. Not wanting it, not NOT wanting it. Just thinking, *Wow . . . That's gonna be weird.*

And that's sort of what this was like.

The second feeling I had was stronger and darker and
creepier.

It was this sadness that enveloped me. And it wasn't
about not being able to have kids. I saved all that hysteria for
later.

Somehow, in the few short weeks since I'd known of its
existence, I had become attached to my cancer. It simply
didn't seem like a foreign entity trying to destroy me. It
seemed more like a part of me that had gotten, well, a little
out of control. A part of me that was also a part of Mike.

I know, weird things go through your mind when you go
through something like this.

I had only one night of major panic, and, in retrospect, it
wasn't so bad. (I had been kind of wondering when the
alarm button would hit.) I was so abnormally nonhysterical
about the whole thing, it almost seemed suspicious.

But then it happened. The shoe filled with dread finally
dropped.

The night before the surgery, as I started to drift off to sleep in the darkness, the image of a scalpel cutting me open, and all my insides being revealed, came to me and just scared the bejeezus out of me. My heart started racing, and my face heated up, and beads of sweat formed on my brow.

I suddenly felt like such a, a . . . body. This sensitive machine that oozed and breathed and that blood ran through, that digested and defecated and saw things and heard things and slept and woke up. All of the reality of this just came bounding down on me like it was a train, chug-a-chug-a-chug-a-chug-a-ing into my forehead. And my aliveness became so real to me. I could hear myself breathe. I could feel my blood racing through my heart. And my heart was beating so fast, and I could feel every beat. And my body felt like a single unit, like every part had a vital role to play. And a part was going to be taken from me and it felt as though every other part of me would feel that difference, that absence of something. And then my heart began racing so fast I thought it was going to burst. My breathing was erratic, and sweat was pouring down my face. I was having a good old classic panic attack.

And thoughts of three things got me through that night: war movies, Mary Tyler Moore, and drugs.

I've never been in a war, but I've seen plenty of war movies, and come on, what about all those wounded people?

Did they sit around sobbing because they'd lost their uterus? Okay, I know that doesn't make sense, but you see where I'm going, right? John Gilbert didn't cry about losing his leg in *The Big Parade*. Ronald Reagan didn't pout about losing both legs in *Kings Row*. And then there's always Timothy Bottoms in *Johnny Got His Gun*, who lost his arms, legs AND face. And yet he carried on.

And while there are plenty of *real* places to find inspiration in life without resorting to the movies, I say, grab your inspiration where you can get it. And for me, it was thinking about these films I'd seen that got me through. Like Edward G. Robinson losing his hand in *Tiger Shark*. Or Kirk Douglas without his finger in *The Big Sky*.

Would Edward G. Robinson or Kirk Douglas have pouted if they'd had hysterectomies? I bet not.

So, I thought about all these characters and I tried to buck up a little.

Then I thought of a quote by Mary Tyler Moore. She once said, ''You can't be brave if only wonderful things happen to you.'' Of course, you have to ask yourself if ''brave'' is a quality you want to have. I know that might sound trite, but I know plenty of people who have conducted their lives insulating themselves from having to exhibit any type of bravery. So, I asked myself, ''Do I want to be brave?'' And I said, ''Okay, if the only other option is to be cowardly. I'm more into anticowardly than out-and-out brave, but if brave is a by-product of avoiding cowardice, then, hey, all right.'' And plus, what about Mary Tyler Moore?

And then I thought about drugs. The morphine that was going to drip drip drip into my veins the next day. And I imagined that warm rushing feeling that would overtake me as the painkiller entered my bloodstream. And it was good. It was very good.

My heart slowed. My breathing became regular. I entered The Calm.

At least for the time being.

Chapter 27
A DOZEN EGGS

I WENT IN AND HAD THE OPERATION AND AFTERWARD the doctor came into the recovery room and said, "Julia, the operation was a big success. We were able to get out all of the tumor that we could see. And we were able to save your ovaries, which is a really good thing, because your ovaries emit these hormones which you need. But we're going to recommend that you get about nine weeks of radiation, so we took the liberty of moving your ovaries up about a foot and a half from their original position so that they would be out of the way of the radiation rays."

I took a moment to imagine my ovaries swimming around my armpits.

I said, "Oh . . . Okay."

The doctor must have seen the look of confusion in my groggy eyes and said, "Don't worry, they work from wherever they are."

"Oh. Great."

Then the doctor said, "Another good thing about hanging on to your ovaries is that if you are at all interested in having a biological child one day, it becomes possible that you still can, even sans uterus."

He continued, "If you're interested in having a child, you still can. We can go in and extract some eggs and then you can mix them with some sperm and have a surrogate mother have the child for you."

Oh, great, now I have to meet a guy and a girl!

Then he said, "Now, if you really are interested in having a biological child, I must tell you that the radiation can actually damage your ovaries even in their new position. So I would recommend that we go in now. We can harvest about twelve eggs."

And I was thinking, *Why twelve? Because . . . they're eggs?*

And he said, ''The only problem is we don't have the medical technology to hold on to the eggs by themselves. They have to be fertilized first and then we can freeze them for up to five years. So basically if you do this, you have to know who your sperm donor is going to be. Now.''

So I said, ''Well, okay. I have been seeing someone for a couple of months and I don't know if now is the exact moment to broach this . . .'' I could just imagine myself saying to Carl the next time he's in town, ''Hey, before the movies on Friday night, why not fertilize all my eggs? 'Cause, you know, things might really work out between us.'' And then I would give him the thumbs-up. And then I'd smile like a maniac.

So then I said to the doctor, ''So, how many different sperm donor people can I have?'' He said, ''Well, I'm not going to allow twelve start-up costs.'' I said, ''Okay, I know, I know. But how many different sperm donors could I have?'' And he said, ''I don't know . . . Six?''

And so I got out my address book, and I thought, *What are the criteria? The criteria are: Someone I know, whose number I have, who I think I could possibly fall in love with one day, and not only fall in love, but we'd want to spend many, many years together. And we'd want to raise a child together and not only raise a child together, but it would have to be our biological child and then we would have to hire a woman to have the child for us.*

So who fits that description?

Chapter 28
MOTHERHOOD DEFERRED

I NEVER IMAGINED THAT, SOMEDAY, I would identify with the barren women of the Old Testament. (I think of a surrogate mother as the modern equivalent of Sarah giving Hagar to Abraham so he could impregnate her. And I remember the story about Rebekah, Isaac's beautiful wife, who was barren until God intervened and opened up her womb.) And I have to admit that I find it a little appealing that those Old Testament guys kept falling for gals who had a difficult time conceiving.

When I was ten, I was obsessed with babies. My mother had my little brother Jim that year, and the teacher of my fourth-grade class even had to have a conference with my parents because I was so distracted by the upcoming arrival of the baby that I couldn't study properly. Forget about memorizing the capitals of the states—I was much more interested in baby clothes.

Sister Norma said that since I couldn't concentrate I might have to be held back. I snuck through that year by the skin of my teeth.

When Jim was born, I spent every minute I could taking care of him. And I began to heavily fantasize about the family of my own that I was going to have someday.

I decided I would have seven kids. That seemed like a reasonable number. Our family, with its meager number of five children, seemed to stand out in my Irish Catholic neighborhood as a little on the paltry side. Almost everyone I knew had seven kids in their family: the Kellys, the Parkers, the McGonigles. Many had more than seven kids: the Driscolls, Condons, the Gales. The Van Veens had sixteen.

So seven seemed to be a conservative number. No one would be asking, "Why so few?" or "Why so many?"

I vividly remember spending one entire day on my single bed upstairs in the T-shaped room imagining delivering my babies. I would writhe in pain, open up my legs, and pretend that I was giving birth. I would give a big push and imagine the nurse handing me my newborn baby, and I'd cry tears of joy. Then I'd rest and do it all again, until my seven babies were born. Like a litter.

Then I began to search for names for my kids, and I filled an entire notebook with my favorites. One day I sat down at my desk and made the final list: Jason, Ellen, Terrence, Joshua, Claire, Matthew, and Colleen.

Then I began to design a house for us to live in. It would have three stories, with a kitchen like this, a TV room like that, and a library, a Ping-Pong room, and an art room and a sewing room. And a Lego room. Oh. And a music room. And a get-away-from-all-the-people room, which would be wallpapered with happy-face stickers (as a ten-year-old in 1970, I couldn't imagine a more soothing and meditative environment).

At Christmas, I would fantasy-shop for the kids in the toy department at The Crescent. I picked out bikes for each one, and the color of the bikes went with the color of their rooms, which went with the color of their hair.

In the summer, I would imagine that we took a huge camper to Glacier National Park for vacation, and I would make my popular tuna sandwiches for lunch (and a special sandwich for Joshua, because he didn't like sweet pickles).

In the fall I would sew all their new "after-school clothes," which I would pick out from the Butterick Pattern Book. (They wouldn't need assorted school clothes for Catholic school, we'd just head down to the Spokane Uniform Shop for those.)

The next year I began to calculate how old each kid would be in relation to one another, the way I did with my own family. My dad would sit on the edge of my bed at night and I would say, "When I'm sixteen, then Meg will be fourteen," or "When Bill is twenty-two, Mike will be twenty." And I could do this for hours.

So, I applied this logic to my own imaginary kids, and that's when they all started growing up in my mind. And before I knew it, they all started going to college.

Colleen wanted to be an architect, so I asked my dad about the best architectural schools. I decided that she would go to Texas for that. Jason was going to be a brain surgeon, so I agreed with myself that the University of Washington Medical School would be fine. Claire was going to play the cello in the symphony, so she'd have to go to New York City (and study at Juilliard, which my dad told me was a famous music school), and Matthew, who was never interested in girls, would naturally enter the priesthood.

So all my kids grew up and went to prestigious universities and became dedicated and successful professionals and none of them ever wavered in what they wanted to do.

Somehow, I did all of this without a husband. I mean, I wasn't a single mother, but for the life of me, I can't remember imagining a husband in all of this. He had no occupation. No personality. And he never got anything for Christmas.

So I think it's not a coincidence that when I turned thirteen or fourteen and began to discover boys, I pretty much forgot about my family. Plus, I grew tired of thinking of them. After all, I had put those seven kids first for years. I think my obsession reached its crescendo when I would fantasize about Terrence going to Europe for his junior year abroad. I suddenly thought, *Hey! How come he gets to go to Europe and I've never been?* I got so upset by this I began to cry.

After that episode, I pretty much stopped thinking about babies. I felt like I'd already *had* a family. And I was thirteen.

After I finished college, my basic attitude about having children was this: Of course I would have them one day, but until then, I had to get a lot of living in. I felt responsible for accumulating as many accomplishments and experiences as I could, so my kids would have the benefit of a mother who was worldly-wise and mature.

But then something happened I didn't figure on.

When I finally did go to Europe, I expected to have a great time and come home with the feeling that I'd done it. That I would now want to settle down and just spend the rest of my life telling my children all about it. But this didn't happen.

Instead, I found out that I *liked* going to Europe. And I began to think about other places I wanted to see: Prague, Moscow, Hong Kong, Osaka. And what about Africa? Peru? and New Zealand?

This same thing happened when it came to work. The more I worked, the more I wanted to work, and the more time I wanted to devote to my work, and so on.

With so much going, how would I ever have time for kids? At the rate I was going, I'd be seventy-three before I had logged enough experience and had done enough good work to feel ready to give it up for those seven babies. It began to dawn on me that all of the terrific life experiences I was having weren't simply to deposit in a savings account I could bequeath to my children—all of this wonderful living was for me.

And that's when I began to consider having children—in an adult way—for the first time.

But then I started to notice all of these people who were happily childless.

This was a big discovery for me. Just the idea of being happily childless. I guess I had been socialized to think that anyone without children had to be depressed about it, or was plagued, or terribly unlucky or something. And the very idea of choosing not to have children, well, that had an air of immorality about it.

And I grew up thinking that people who didn't have children were the type who would go out and carouse in bars all night, dancing on the tabletops, tossing money in the air while they threw their heads back in raucous laughter. But as I got older, I began to realize that those people were the type of people who *did* have children.

The other myth that started exploding in my head was the idea that people who chose not to have children didn't like them, like the witch in ''Hansel and Gretel'' or W. C. Fields.

Luckily, I had grand examples of fulfilled, happy, childless people all around me. My mother's two sisters never had children, and they didn't appear to be moping around feeling as though they'd missed out on something essential to their happiness. In fact, they seemed happier than most people, and they definitely loved children.

And being raised Catholic, I had nuns as an example, too. Those women were careerists who were dedicated and spiritual and loved children, and they didn't have them, and they had chosen not to.

And of course, I have many friends who are childless—by choice—and they don't find that simply because they've chosen not to pass on their DNA, their lives lack value.

So I started to actually flirt with the idea that I might not have children. I tried it on for size and it seemed to fit okay. There were even advantages: I could moan about the population problem without feeling any guilt, and I could conjure up dire images of the future of civilization, without being fearful for my offspring. And thinking like this made life seem longer and more relaxed.

But then two things happened that changed everything: I met someone, fell in love, and wanted to have everything with him—including children. I finally made that connection that I couldn't make at age ten.

And I got cancer and had my uterus removed.

Both of these developments threw a serious wrench into my mix.

I finally had to accept the fact that I was never going to be pregnant: I will never get to have my spouse put his hand on my swollen belly, great with child. I will never have someone rush ahead of me and grab my shopping bags because ''I shouldn't be carrying anything heavy and I should get off my feet.'' I will never eat for two. And I know I'll miss the experience of actually giving birth, which is something that I've always looked forward to, despite the pain, just for the sheer miracle of it.

But if that's my heaviest cross to bear, it seems like such a light one.

Don't get me wrong, I spent plenty of moments in anguish coming to terms with my reality, but sometimes it's in your limitations that you find your greatest strengths.

I began to realize that I have no overwhelming emotional need to have my specific genetic code continue after me. Not that I'm ashamed of it or anything, but I don't feel like my DNA has something going for it over anyone else's. And, at the risk of sounding like an ad for an adoption agency, there really are just too many children out there who need parents, and I believe that adoption can bring a child and a parent together in a way that is seriously spiritual and totally valuable. And that's cool.

So, I figure I'm in a good space. I can still raise a child, although I can't bear one, and in a corny way, I'm glad that my own medical struggle has forced me to answer some deeper questions that I might have otherwise just skimmed over or avoided completely.

And that makes this cross of mine feel like a feather.

Chapter 29
MOM AND DAD, GO HOME!

WELL, I CAME HOME FROM THE HOSPITAL and my parents were there, eager to help me in any way. I was in a tremendous amount of pain, but I tried not to take the painkillers that my physicians had prescribed for me. I just figured, if I could endure the pain on my own, or if I could do that thing where you visualize the pain and then encompass it, and then transcend it, I would really enjoy those Percodan a lot more later with a margarita.

Now, after you have a hysterectomy or any abdominal surgery, the name of the game is to keep fluid running through you. You have to drink a lot of liquid and you have to go to the bathroom and keep a chart and, well, it's just pretty awful.

And one day I was in the bathroom and my mother was on the other side of the closed door and she yelled in, ''Julie, did you go yet?'' And I said, ''Uh, yeah . . .'' And she said, ''Good girl!'' And as I was sitting there on the toilet, I thought, *You know, I think* this *is my lowest moment.*

I finally recovered sufficiently for my parents to be persuaded to go home. This was partly because my friend David, the one who introduced me to his brother Carl, had decided to move down from Aspen and help see me through the radiation.

And so my parents packed up all of their bags and then loaded up the car. And you know, my parents have always been either a source of comedy or a reason to be in therapy for me.

I'd always thought of them as being really provincial and kind of wacky and I always jumped on the dysfunctional family bandwagon. But it wasn't until that year when the shit really hit the fan that I saw how really functional they ultimately are.

And when I think of the hundreds of images that I now have in my head, of my father filling out Social Security forms late into the night or my mother whipping up Jell-O for Mike in the kitchen or each of them taking one of Mike's arms when he was too weak to walk to the car by himself, I think how horrible it must have been to have brought a child into this world only to have to help him out again . . .

As the car drove away I realized that my feelings for them had deepened so much.

Chapter 30
FIRE-STOP

DAVID MOVED INTO THE NOW-VACANT guest room for the big radiation extravaganza. Every morning at 8:45 we went to Cedars Sinai so I could get my radiation and David would wait for me in the waiting room just like I had for Mike. And when I would come out, I'm sure I had an oddly amused expression on my face and our eyes would meet and we'd laugh that little laugh like ''How weird is this?''

It was so strange to suddenly be on the other side of this experience; it almost felt like Mike and I and David were square-dancing.

When you have someone pass away that's as close to you as Mike was to me, it's almost like the synapses in your brain don't all get the message at once. And especially in that first moment of waking, it's like, you forget that they died.

This one morning I woke up and I walked down the hallway and my eyes caught a glimpse of a picture of Mike and his best friend Andy in Hawaii, and it was as if I had just heard that Mike died. And I wanted to run down the hallway and bang on David's bedroom door and yell, ''Mike died! Mike died!'' But I didn't. I just burst into tears and I started crying and David got up and I was really sobbing, uncontrollably, and he didn't know what to do to try to help me.

So, eventually, he decided to try to help me based on this applied theory of the fire-stop. A fire-stop is basically this: When a forest fire is burning out of control, sometimes they burn this ring around the outside of it so that when the fire reaches the dead area, it naturally comes to a stop. And for David to apply this theory to me meant that we immediately had to go see the movie *The Bridges of Madison County*.

It was the day that *Bridges* opened and there David and I were in line for the very first matinee: me already crying. And sure enough, during the movie, at just that moment when everyone in the theater burst into tears and started crying, I stopped crying and didn't cry again for another week.

Chapter 31
SISTER ANTONELLA

IT TURNED OUT THAT MY RADIATION THERAPIST was from Spokane. And coincidentally she had also gone to my old high school, Marycliff. But we didn't know each other because she was a few years ahead of me.

We'd both been taught by Sister Antonella and so we'd reminisce about her. Sister Antonella was the stern English teacher at my all-girls Catholic high school who was reviled by many and beloved by a few. I was one of the latter.

She was a strict disciplinarian and it was my first chance to be taught by someone who treated me like an adult and didn't talk down to me about literature. We read Thoreau,

Shelley, and a ton of Shakespeare. (A ton for a freshman in high school being *Macbeth* and *Romeo and Juliet*.)

Sometimes she would invite me to have dinner with the other nuns at the convent, which was a late-nineteenth-century mansion. She showed me their rooms with the elaborate molding of cherubs and flowers, and the enormous closets that were now empty, except for the single habit on an old wire hanger. I couldn't imagine anything more glamorous than living there.

She was the debate coach and I immediately signed up for the team. The first year our topic was ''Should OPEC be obliterated?'' The second year it was ''Should the Electoral College be abolished?'' I guess at that time debaters were interested in arguing about demolishing institutions.

So my radiation therapist and I would talk about Sister Antonella while I would get up onto the radiation bed and position myself correctly so the radiation machine could circle my abdomen and send lethal rays into tiny exact spots on my body.

I asked her if she knew what had ever happened to Sister Antonella. She said she'd heard that she was on an Indian reservation in Montana, teaching the children there. And so then I'd think about her, and wonder how the children were taking her.

I remembered when Sister Antonella had taught us Emerson. She made us memorize the quote "Give me health and a day and I will make the pomp of emperors ridiculous."

Chapter 32
LOST OVARIES

ONE DAY MY RADIATION DOCTOR SAID, "Julia, I'm afraid we have some bad news." I said, "Oh, bad news." He said, "It appears that we've lost one of your ovaries," and I said, "Oh, you know my oncologist warned me about that. He said one of my ovaries might die from the effect of the radiation, so don't worry, I was prepared."

And my doctor said, "No, no, no, I don't mean that one of your ovaries has died. I mean, we've lost one of your ovaries. We've been looking at these X rays . . ." And then he turned toward this big X ray of my midsection that was hanging on the lighted wall behind him. He continued while he brushed his hands all over my innards, "You can see this one,'' and then he pointed to a little round glob about the size of a dime that seemed lodged next to my stomach. And then he said, "But the other one's gone off somewhere.'' And then he threw his hands up in the air, like he was Columbo.

I said, "Oh, wow.'' And I sat down, suddenly feeling guilty that I had such a rebellious ovary. Then he tried to comfort me and said, "You know, I've seen this before, and it's not unusual for an ovary, once cut off from its responsibilities, to travel.''

Now, I suppose I understand that. If I were an ovary and I suddenly didn't have to deal with that fallopian tube anymore, I'd probably want to go around and see some stuff.

I said, "I guess what we are looking for here is the anatomical equivalent to Florida.''

The doctor said, "Don't worry, it's going to turn up eventually." And I said, "Now, I'm not going to, like, cough it up, am I?''

He said, "No, that's pretty much impossible.''

Chapter 33
JESUS AND THE HOUSE IS EMPTY

MY RADIATION CAME TO AN END, and my energy was re-
stored, and David moved back to Aspen.

And you know, I talk to my parents much more fre-
quently than I did before this whole ordeal. My mother says
that she finds herself driving up to Holy Cross Cemetery all
the time to visit Mike. She'll be running an errand downtown and she'll find herself absentmindedly driving toward
the cemetery. She's also doing a lot more volunteer work at
my parents' parish. She's part of this women's auxiliary
group there. And a few months ago she called me and said,

"Julie, you know the Ladies' Auxiliary has been meeting and we have all agreed that . . . you know the Jesus that is up on the altar at church? Well, he has such a . . . sad look on his face, and he's just so . . . depressing-looking. So we all decided that we'd like a new Jesus! Well, we told Monsignor and, Julie, Monsignor chose *me* to pick the new Jesus! So he gave me a catalog where you order those things from Europe and whatnot and I went through it and I'm telling you, Julie, one Jesus was just sadder than the next! But then I got to the last page and I found my Jesus! Well he's got long, blond, gorgeous curls and these legs that just . . . are very long! And he's very muscular and it's almost like he's . . ." she lowered her voice an octave and whispered, "bench-pressing that cross up there . . . I showed him to the ladies and we have all agreed that we wouldn't mind looking at him for an hour every Sunday! And so we ordered him and he's up and, Julie, I call him my Sports Connection Jesus!"

As you can imagine, things have slowed down considerably back at my house. After I finished my radiation treatment, my black cat, Rita, miraculously grew back all of her fur. And one day I opened the door and Gus walked in like he'd been walking in every single day. And he stayed.

I still get a lot of mail for Mike. Mike subscribed to a lot of different periodicals, some of which are starting to lapse. And one of them is to *Buzz* magazine. In the last several months I've gotten two of those computer-generated notices for Mike, one that said, ''Hey, Mike! Where'd ya go?'' And the next one said, ''Mike Sweeney, where've you been?''

And I finally, finally have my house all to myself. And you know what? I really, really love it. But sometimes, when I sit there, I wonder, *Why does it feel so empty?*

Chapter 34
TAKING THE ROCK BACK

A FEW WEEKS LATER, QUENTIN AND I were on the phone comparing our years.

You see, before my year from hell, Quentin and I would routinely talk about our hopes and dreams. Then, as the year progressed, I watched Quentin realize all of his. And, in total honesty, it was a joy to see someone so deserving get so much. And, of course, I have to admit that I loved the dark hellish comedy of the whole thing. "Hi! Congrats on the Academy Awards! That's quite an achievement!" "Thanks. But how's your cancer?" "Oh, worse, I'm bleeding from the radiation, but enough about that, how's your girlfriend?" And then I would have to fall into spasms of laughter. Finally, Quentin said, ''We're taking that damn rock back.''

The rock had sat passively, but apparently angrily, on my mantel for the entire year. When I would dust, I always paused for a moment at the rock. And being one who is completely unsuperstitious, it nagged at me.

So we left for Ireland in August. On Quentin's dime. And first-class too. And it was heaven.

So much had happened since our trip just one year before. Michael O'Donoghue, whom we'd gone to see with his wife, Cheryl, had died suddenly of a brain aneurysm three months after our first trip to Ireland. It was horrible and shocking and came without warning. The last time I had spoken with him was from a bank of pay phones in the hospital in Rochester. Michael O'Donoghue had gone to college in Rochester, and he shared the most scathingly funny, and yet sentimental, anecdotes about the city. He was empathetic, bitingly droll, and informational: my three favorite qualities in a person.

Not long after that, he woke up one day with a headache, and by 5:00 P.M. he was dead.

And so now, as Cheryl was packing up the house in Ireland, Quentin and I were returning for our last hurrah.

Quentin didn't take his rock back. He figured if there was any type of luck change associated with the possession of the rock, he was going to hold on to his.

There was a big group of us there, including several of Cheryl and Michael's Irish and American friends. We all holed up in the big house for a week and partied like I'd never partied before. It went on day and night and we decided that we would go, en masse, back out to Inish Turk and make a kind of ceremony out of me returning that rock.

And once there, after much champagne and salmon and soda bread, we rose and carried the rock on a blanket with dried flowers, herbs, and Quentin's cigar, like it was the King of Siam. We marched across to the other side of the island and I flung the rock back over the cliff, back down among its kind.

I didn't want to make such a big deal of it, or to give in to the truth of the curse, but I have to admit, as I saw that white rock sail through the sky, so individual against the green and blue backdrop of water and land, and then fall onto the shoreline, where I was unable to distinguish it in the white sea of a million broken stones, something in me felt released.

P.S. Carl and I are still together.

So far, so good. Okay. Extremely good.

PICTURE NOTES

CONTENTS • Us Sweeney kids skiing at Schweitzer, Idaho, Christmas, 1994.

PROLOGUE • Daisy Fuentes and me in Hawaii, 1994.

CHAPTER 1 • Quentin Tarantino and me in Ireland, 1994.

CHAPTER 2 • Sweeney siblings (sans Jim), childhood, 1966.

CHAPTER 3 • Our actual *Nunsense* ticket stub.

CHAPTER 4 • My living room in Shangri-la.

CHAPTER 5 • Jim, me, and Mike, 1989.

CHAPTER 6 • Mike in Hawaii, 1993.

CHAPTER 7 • Jeri Sweeney, Christmas every year.

CHAPTER 8 • Bob Sweeney, head shot for his role in *It's Pat*, 1992.

CHAPTER 9 • Dad, Mom, and me, Puerto Vallarta, 1995.

CHAPTER 10 • Mike, Dad, and Mom, outside Shangri-la, 1994.

CHAPTER 11 • Gus taking a drink. • Frank hiding behind the books. • Rita looks like a demon by the scratching post.

CHAPTER 12 • Pat, picture taken by Edie Baskin at *SNL*, 1990.

CHAPTER 13 • Mike getting radiation at the UCLA Comprehensive Cancer Center, 1994.

CHAPTER 14 • The Pope. Copyright © by Bernard Bisson/ Sygma.

CHAPTER 15 • Still from *In a Lonely Place,* Humphrey Bogart and the hatcheck girl, 1950.

CHAPTER 16 ▪ Carl, self-portrait, 1987.

CHAPTER 17 ▪ Mike with friends Sharon and Julie, Thanksgiving, 1994.

CHAPTER 18 ▪ Still from *I Know Where I'm Going*, Roger Livesey and Wendy Hiller, 1945.

CHAPTER 19 ▪ Mike and me at El Coyote, 1992.

CHAPTER 20 ▪ A totally staged picture of my coffee with Dr. Fu, 1997.

CHAPTER 21 ▪ Dad and Mom while visiting Meg in Japan, 1993.

CHAPTER 22 ▪ Mike and me at El Coyote, 1992.

CHAPTER 23 ▪ Where Santa Monica meets Beverly, Los Angeles.

CHAPTER 24 ▪ Mike's head shot, 1993.

CHAPTER 25 ▪ This isn't Father Fitterer, it's Monsignor Buckley. I didn't have a picture of Father Fitterer, so I figured Monsignor Buckley would have to do.

CHAPTER 26 ▪ Me and Dad in my hospital room after the hysterectomy, 1995. (I know . . . he loves that sweatshirt!)

CHAPTER 27 ▪ Eggs.

CHAPTER 28 ▪ Me and my nephew Nick Sweeney, 1993.

CHAPTER 29 ▪ The Toyota is packed, 1995.

CHAPTER 30 ▪ David Frank and me during the summer of radiation, 1995.

CHAPTER 31 ▪ Sister Antonella, c. 1974.

CHAPTER 32 ▪ Cruise ship. Copyright © by Brooks Kraft/ Sygma.

CHAPTER 33 ▪ Piano top inside my house, 1996.

CHAPTER 34 ▪ The rock with its offerings, Ireland, 1996.